Woman's Day
Dictionary of Antique Furniture

Woman's Day
Dictionary
of Antique
Furniture

Edith Gaines AND *Dorothy H. Jenkins*

Illustrated by Helen Disbrow and Charles Reiger

HAWTHORN BOOKS, INC.
Publishers / New York
A Howard & Wyndham Company

WOMAN'S DAY DICTIONARY OF ANTIQUE FURNITURE

Copyright © 1974 Fawcett Publications Inc. Copyright © 1965, 1966, 1967 Fawcett Publications Inc. Copyright under International and Pan-American Copyright Conventions. All rights reserved, including the right to reproduce this book or portions thereof in any form, except for the inclusion of brief quotations in a review. All inquiries should be addressed to Fawcett Publications Inc., CBS Consumer Publications, 1515 Broadway, New York, New York 10036. This book was manufactured in the United States of America and published simultaneously in Canada by Prentice-Hall of Canada, Limited, 1870 Birchmount Road, Scarborough, Ontario.

Library of Congress Catalog Card Number: 78–61643

ISBN: 0–8015–8792–1

2 3 4 5 6 7 8 9 10

Published by arrangement with CBS Consumer Publications, A Division of CBS Inc.

Contents

Woman's Day
Dictionary of Antique Furniture

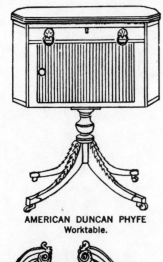

AMERICAN DUNCAN PHYFE
Worktable.

AMERICAN QUEEN ANNE
Lowboy.

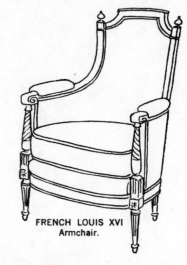

FRENCH LOUIS XVI
Armchair.

AMERICAN CHIPPENDALE
Highboy.

Written and edited by **EDITH GAINES**
Associate Editor of Antiques *Magazine*

Illustrated by **HELEN DISBROW**

Furnishing a home is something that all women look forward to at some point in their lives. And whether it be a ranch house, a Cape Cod cottage or a three-room apartment, a knowledge of furniture is essential. By developing a familiarity with periods and styles you will be a better judge of what to choose in order to give your home the kind of character that will best suit you and your family. The more you know about the past, the better judge you will be of the present. A knowledge of periods and styles will add a great deal to your understanding and enjoyment of furniture. With your added knowledge will come a new appreciation of our national historic restorations and a new zest for poking around in antique shops or country barns and in attending neighborhood auctions. The WOMAN'S DAY DICTIONARY OF FURNITURE, by grouping the most important forms in every style, shows you the outstanding characteristic of each, makes it possible for you to understand the derivation of modern furniture and to judge the authenticity of reproductions. It may also lead you to discover some gems in your attic that you can restore and refinish. And, finally, in a historic house, a museum, a friend's home or your own, you will be surprised to find out how much fun it is to know what you are looking at.

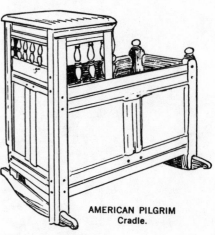

AMERICAN PILGRIM
Cradle.

AMERICAN HEPPLEWHITE
Secretary.

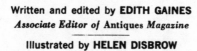

ENGLISH QUEEN ANNE
Side chair.

The European Background

ENGLISH

DICTIONARY OF FURNITURE

ENGLISH

Jacobean court cupboard for display of silver or pewter. Oak; melon-bulb supports.

Restoration fall-front secretary. Marquetry; spiral turnings.

William and Mary chest of drawers. Walnut with oyster inlay; large ball feet.

Early Georgian chest-on-chest. Broken pediment top, fluted columns.

Queen Anne secretary. Arched panels, broken-arch top; slant-front desk; bracket feet.

Chippendale chest of drawers in the "French taste." Rococo shape and carving; French-scroll feet.

Chippendale break-front secretary. Mahogany; paneling, broken-pediment top, simple flush cabinet base.

Adam console, made to stand against wall. Demilune shape; painted in pastels and inlaid.

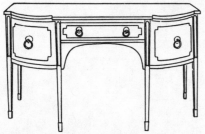

Hepplewhite sideboard. Mahogany; shaped front; string (narrow line) inlay; pendent ring handles and tapered legs with spade feet.

Sheraton secretary-bookcase with mirror door. Mahogany and satinwood.

Regency cabinet in "classical" design. Rosewood; paneled; elaborate brass appliqué trim.

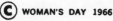

ENGLISH furniture styles seem quite familiar to Americans because from the beginning most of our own furniture was made after English models, by men trained in English techniques. JACOBEAN furniture (1600-1660) is still semi-medieval: simple, heavy, with little concession to comfort. Most of it is made of oak. The RESTORATION style (1660-1690) is considerably more sophisticated, showing, in spiral turnings, fancy stretchers and Flemish scrolls, the influence of the cabinetmakers Charles II brought with him when he returned from exile on the Continent; walnut is now the most popular wood. WILLIAM AND MARY pieces (1690-1700) reflect the taste of a king imported from Holland and are apt to have a no-nonsense solidity. In the graceful QUEEN ANNE designs (1700-1715) comfort is for the first time paramount. EARLY GEORGIAN (1715-1750), rich and ornate, shows the effect of increasing national prosperity; an architectural note is added. CHIPPENDALE (1740-1765) keeps the architectural but adds variety: it introduces the "French taste," follows the vogue for chinoiserie. With ADAM (1765-1795), classic motifs from ancient Greece and Italy appear, the result of renewed interest in the ancient world. These are apparent also in the light and delicate furniture called HEPPLEWHITE (1775-1800) and SHERATON (1790-1810). The somewhat heavier REGENCY style (1795-1820), emphasizing dark woods and metal trim, echoes the French Directoire and Empire modes and appealed strongly to the rising class of wealthy businessmen.

14

Jacobean paneled oak (wainscot) armchair. Gouge or chisel carving.

Restoration chair. Caning; Flemish scrolls.

William and Mary armchair. Walnut; serpentine X-stretcher.

Queen Anne two-chair-back settee. Walnut; scrolled arm, cabriole leg, pad foot.

Early Georgian armchair. Gilt and velvet; carved leg and arm supports.

Chippendale chair. Mahogany and leather; carved crest and splat.

Adam armchair in French style. Carved, fluted; pastel satin.

Hepplewhite shield-back armchair. Tapered leg, receding arm support.

Sheraton armchair. Roman motif; arm supports and legs turned and reeded.

Regency bench. Carved and gilded; copy of Roman curule form.

Jacobean drop-leaf table. Oak; turned legs, box stretcher.

Restoration side table. Flat curved X-stretcher, spiral turned legs with bun feet; marquetry trim.

William and Mary lowboy. Trumpet legs, shaped skirt.

Queen Anne drop-leaf table. Walnut; straight legs, pad feet.

Chippendale china table. Mahogany, marble top; claw-and-ball feet.

Early Georgian side table. Carved and gilded pine; carvings include shells, leaves, blossoms, fruit, birds' heads.

Hepplewhite sewing table. Splayed legs.

Sheraton sofa table. Satinwood; spirally reeded legs and stretcher, brass casters.

Regency drum table. Tripod base, hexagonal pillar, paw feet.

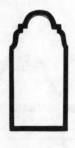

William and Mary looking glass. Inlaid.

Queen Anne. Molded frame, arched and scrolled top.

Early Georgian. Carved and gilt; broken pediment.

Chippendale. Gilt and gesso; asymmetric rococo carving.

Hepplewhite. Classical urn-and-flower motifs.

Sheraton. Architectural elements; painted, gilded.

Regency. Gilt frame, convex glass.

WOMAN'S DAY DICTIONARY OF
18th-Century
ENGLISH FURNITURE
BY
DOROTHY H. JENKINS

QUEEN ANNE table with one drop leaf is walnut; known as a handkerchief, corner or triangular table. Circa 1710.

CHIPPENDALE candlestand is mahogany with fretwork support and gallery. 1755-1760.

SHERATON commode, harewood and satinwood; inlaid, painted. Circa 1795.

EARLY GEORGIAN side table is mahogany with marble top; cabriole legs are carved. Circa 1730.

HEPPLEWHITE armchair has beechwood frame with shield-shaped back; seat is upholstered. Circa 1780.

MID-GEORGIAN commode in French manner, mahogany; gilt-bronze hoof feet. Circa 1765.

MID-GEORGIAN armchair by Robert Adam has carved and gilded frame. Circa 1760.

EARLY GEORGIAN mirror has gilded wood frame carved with classical motifs. Circa 1720.

MID-GEORGIAN bureau-desk with cylinder top is made of inlaid satinwood. Circa 1790.

AMERICAN CHIPPENDALE tip-and-turn table, piecrust edge. 1755-1780.

Beauty of line and ornament, lustrous woods, and workmanship that has never been surpassed distinguish the furniture in which England took pride between 1700 and 1800. This great, restless century, which brought immense changes to the world, opened new vistas to English furniture designers and craftsmen. The fashions that they set have long survived them to become known as the traditional eighteenth-century styles. Bold exploration and trade brought into good supply the two fashionable woods of the century, walnut and mahogany. By 1700 English furniture craftsmen had learned the techniques of veneering, marquetry and inlay; these had been introduced after the Restoration in 1660 brought the monarchy back from exile in France. Travel on the Continent aroused interest in classical styles, first along the lines of Italy's sixteenth-century architect, Andrea Palladio, and then, starting about 1760, with the delicate ornament used by the ancient Romans. The greatly admired imports from China led to fretwork and japanning.

Despite these diverse influences in the 1700's, English furniture for the first time was made for comfort and convenience. Variety entered with bookcases for the books now common in many homes and china cabinets for porcelain from the Far East, to mention only two of the new pieces.

This century also was the age of designers, whose ideas were disseminated in America and throughout the world by trade and pattern book.

Illustrations by HELEN DISBROW

MORE ▶

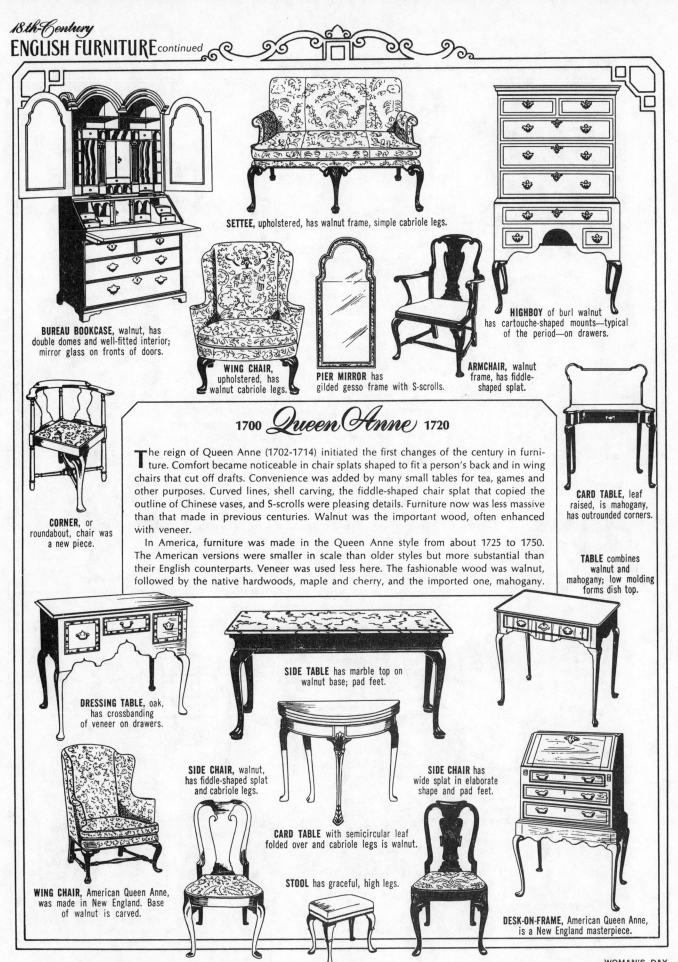

BUREAU BOOKCASE, walnut, has double domes and well-fitted interior; mirror glass on fronts of doors.

SETTEE, upholstered, has walnut frame, simple cabriole legs.

HIGHBOY of burl walnut has cartouche-shaped mounts—typical of the period—on drawers.

WING CHAIR, upholstered, has walnut cabriole legs.

PIER MIRROR has gilded gesso frame with S-scrolls.

ARMCHAIR, walnut frame, has fiddle-shaped splat.

CORNER, or roundabout, chair was a new piece.

1700 *Queen Anne* 1720

The reign of Queen Anne (1702-1714) initiated the first changes of the century in furniture. Comfort became noticeable in chair splats shaped to fit a person's back and in wing chairs that cut off drafts. Convenience was added by many small tables for tea, games and other purposes. Curved lines, shell carving, the fiddle-shaped chair splat that copied the outline of Chinese vases, and S-scrolls were pleasing details. Furniture now was less massive than that made in previous centuries. Walnut was the important wood, often enhanced with veneer.

In America, furniture was made in the Queen Anne style from about 1725 to 1750. The American versions were smaller in scale than older styles but more substantial than their English counterparts. Veneer was used less here. The fashionable wood was walnut, followed by the native hardwoods, maple and cherry, and the imported one, mahogany.

CARD TABLE, leaf raised, is mahogany, has outrounded corners.

TABLE combines walnut and mahogany; low molding forms dish top.

DRESSING TABLE, oak, has crossbanding of veneer on drawers.

SIDE TABLE has marble top on walnut base; pad feet.

SIDE CHAIR, walnut, has fiddle-shaped splat and cabriole legs.

CARD TABLE with semicircular leaf folded over and cabriole legs is walnut.

SIDE CHAIR has wide splat in elaborate shape and pad feet.

WING CHAIR, American Queen Anne, was made in New England. Base of walnut is carved.

STOOL has graceful, high legs.

DESK-ON-FRAME, American Queen Anne, is a New England masterpiece.

CONSOLE, a table placed bracketlike against a wall, has gilded support, marble top.

CANDLESTAND, walnut, has tripod base and octagonal top.

SETTEE, one of a pair, has gilded beechwood frame with carving of shell, scroll and acanthus leaf.

DRESSING TABLE, mahogany, has scrolled apron and cabriole legs.

1720 *Early Georgian* 1760

Prosperity accompanied by creative energy and constant change marked the reigns of George I (1714–1727) and George II (1727–1760). London became the center for importing the essential materials and exporting furniture. The second quarter of the century brought to the fore William Kent, who designed furniture for houses built in the English Palladian style of architecture, which had been introduced about 1719. Kent excelled as a furniture designer and set a sumptuous style in interior decoration. Side tables with marble tops were typical of Kent's massive pieces of furniture, all of which were given baroque treatment with extravagant carving of scrolls and swags, often painted and gilded. By mid-century, other designers and cabinetmakers in London brought to prominence Gothic, Chinese and the rococo or French styles. Carving continued to be opulent. The cabriole leg ending in claw-and-ball foot had been introduced in the Queen Anne period; during the Early Georgian years, this style of front leg that curved outward at the knee and inward above the foot was carved lavishly and terminated in either a claw-and-ball or a club foot. The solid splat in chair backs was replaced by a carved, open design. Walnut began to go out of fashion in London about 1735; its successor was mahogany. This handsome wood was imported in increasingly large quantity after heavy import duties were abolished in 1721.

CARD TABLE with leaf down is richly carved, especially on the cabriole legs.

TABLE, mahogany, has two drop leaves and simple cabriole legs without carving.

ARMCHAIR, one of a pair, has carved walnut frame, upholstered seat.

ARMCHAIR, upholstered, has four cabriole legs; front legs are carved with acanthus leaf.

STOOL, mahogany with fabric top, has scrolled aprons and cabriole legs.

MIRROR in walnut frame has crest carving of three feathers, a heraldic badge of the Prince of Wales.

LIBRARY TABLE by William Kent displays baroque decoration in paw feet, lion head terminals and shells.

ARMCHAIR, mahogany, has latticework back in Chinese style.

READING OR "STRADDLE" CHAIR was a gentleman's favorite; this one is mahogany and leather.

SIDE CHAIR combines Queen Anne back with Georgian carving.

DESK has two pedestals of drawers; walnut with walnut veneer as ornament.

SIDE TABLE in the baroque style of William Kent has marble top on elaborately carved base of gilded pine.

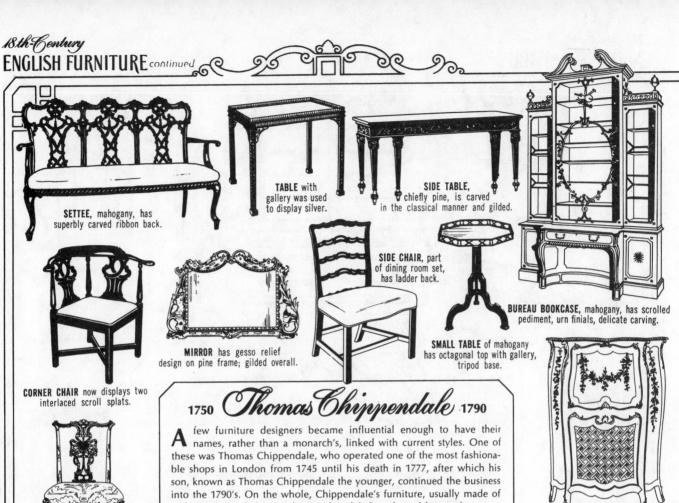

SETTEE, mahogany, has superbly carved ribbon back.

TABLE with gallery was used to display silver.

SIDE TABLE, chiefly pine, is carved in the classical manner and gilded.

SIDE CHAIR, part of dining room set, has ladder back.

MIRROR has gesso relief design on pine frame; gilded overall.

CORNER CHAIR now displays two interlaced scroll splats.

SMALL TABLE of mahogany has octagonal top with gallery, tripod base.

BUREAU BOOKCASE, mahogany, has scrolled pediment, urn finials, delicate carving.

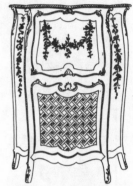

CABINET of dark kingwood has elaborate marquetry decoration.

SIDE CHAIR with ribbon back follows design in Chippendale's book.

SIDE TABLE has inlaid satinwood top on a carved and gilded base.

1750 *Thomas Chippendale* 1790

A few furniture designers became influential enough to have their names, rather than a monarch's, linked with current styles. One of these was Thomas Chippendale, who operated one of the most fashionable shops in London from 1745 until his death in 1777, after which his son, known as Thomas Chippendale the younger, continued the business into the 1790's. On the whole, Chippendale's furniture, usually made of mahogany, was lighter and more fanciful than that of his predecessors. The publication of his book *The Gentleman and Cabinet-Maker's Director* in 1754 and its subsequent editions in 1755 and 1762 as well as its translation into several languages made Chippendale known worldwide. His name was synonymous with rococo in furniture although he worked in other distinct styles.

The rococo style was borrowed from the French Louis XV furniture, which had graceful curving lines, lavish though delicate decoration. Chippendale's rococo style was embellished by the shell motif. The chinoiserie influence in the 1740's led him to use fretwork, pagoda tops and bamboo turnings as decoration. Fretwork, the pointed arches and quatrefoils of the Gothic revival, marquetry and lacquer were skillful adornments; carving was deep and excellent. Chippendale's mastery shows in handsome chair backs. Although he has been accused of being primarily a manufacturer, there is ample evidence that he was equally successful at designing furniture. Thomas Chippendale the younger is remembered for the distinguished pieces produced in the early 1790's.

ARMCHAIR has mahogany frame distinguished for its carving, particularly the lyre back.

Thomas Chippendale the younger

SIDEBOARD, satinwood, has inlay of grapes on frieze.

COMMODE with bow front is mahogany with inlay in contrasting color.

WRITING TABLE, mahogany, displays boldly simple inlay.

MIRROR, one of a pair, has carved and gilded frame, phoenix crest.

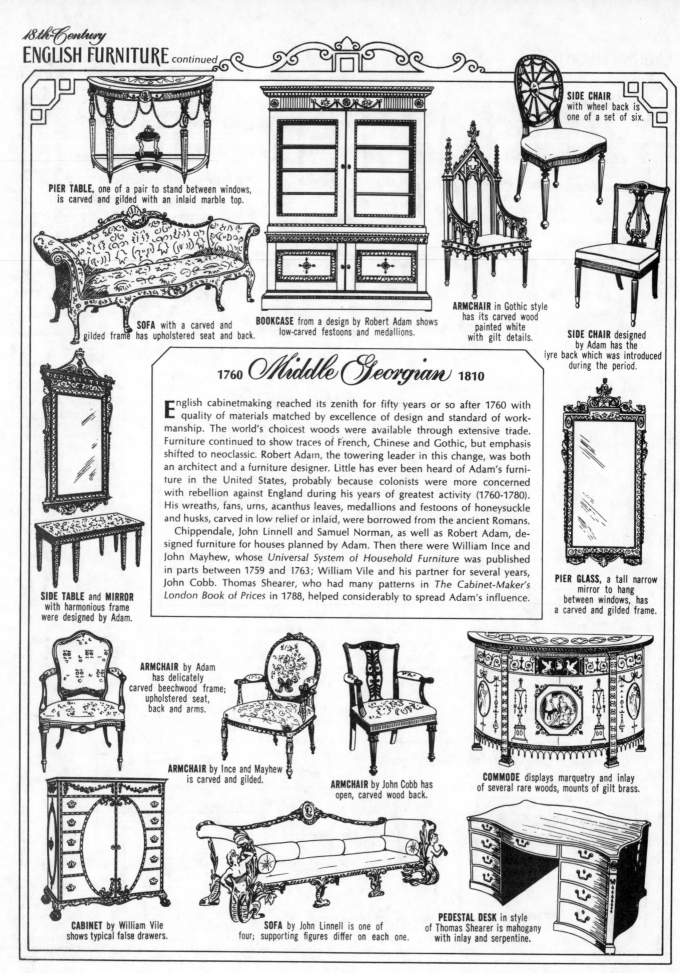

PIER TABLE, one of a pair to stand between windows, is carved and gilded with an inlaid marble top.

SOFA with a carved and gilded frame has upholstered seat and back.

BOOKCASE from a design by Robert Adam shows low-carved festoons and medallions.

ARMCHAIR in Gothic style has its carved wood painted white with gilt details.

SIDE CHAIR with wheel back is one of a set of six.

SIDE CHAIR designed by Adam has the lyre back which was introduced during the period.

SIDE TABLE and **MIRROR** with harmonious frame were designed by Adam.

1760 *Middle Georgian* 1810

English cabinetmaking reached its zenith for fifty years or so after 1760 with quality of materials matched by excellence of design and standard of workmanship. The world's choicest woods were available through extensive trade. Furniture continued to show traces of French, Chinese and Gothic, but emphasis shifted to neoclassic. Robert Adam, the towering leader in this change, was both an architect and a furniture designer. Little has ever been heard of Adam's furniture in the United States, probably because colonists were more concerned with rebellion against England during his years of greatest activity (1760-1780). His wreaths, fans, urns, acanthus leaves, medallions and festoons of honeysuckle and husks, carved in low relief or inlaid, were borrowed from the ancient Romans.

Chippendale, John Linnell and Samuel Norman, as well as Robert Adam, designed furniture for houses planned by Adam. Then there were William Ince and John Mayhew, whose *Universal System of Household Furniture* was published in parts between 1759 and 1763; William Vile and his partner for several years, John Cobb. Thomas Shearer, who had many patterns in *The Cabinet-Maker's London Book of Prices* in 1788, helped considerably to spread Adam's influence.

PIER GLASS, a tall narrow mirror to hang between windows, has a carved and gilded frame.

ARMCHAIR by Adam has delicately carved beechwood frame; upholstered seat, back and arms.

ARMCHAIR by Ince and Mayhew is carved and gilded.

ARMCHAIR by John Cobb has open, carved wood back.

COMMODE displays marquetry and inlay of several rare woods, mounts of gilt brass.

CABINET by William Vile shows typical false drawers.

SOFA by John Linnell is one of four; supporting figures differ on each one.

PEDESTAL DESK in style of Thomas Shearer is mahogany with inlay and serpentine.

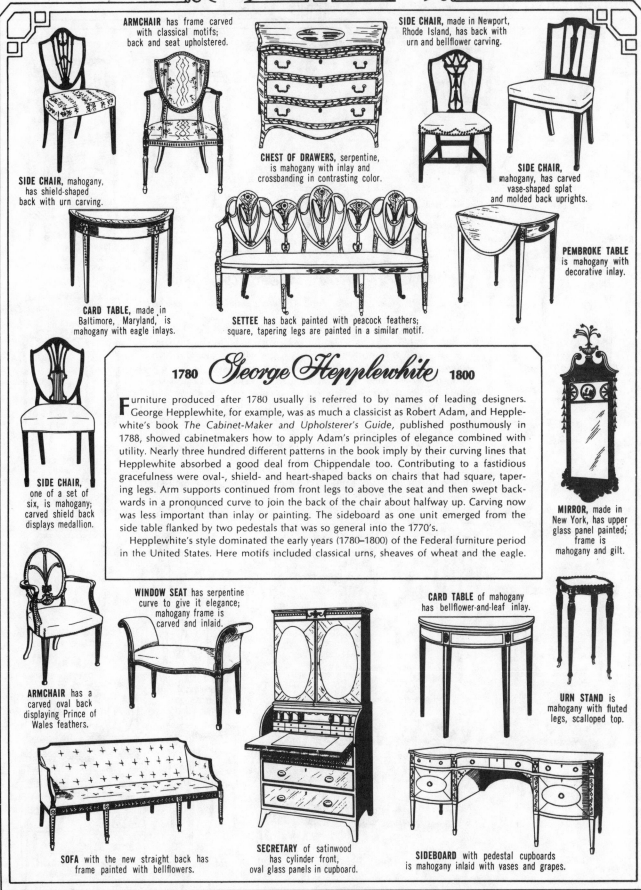

ARMCHAIR has frame carved with classical motifs; back and seat upholstered.

SIDE CHAIR, made in Newport, Rhode Island, has back with urn and bellflower carving.

CHEST OF DRAWERS, serpentine, is mahogany with inlay and crossbanding in contrasting color.

SIDE CHAIR, mahogany, has shield-shaped back with urn carving.

SIDE CHAIR, mahogany, has carved vase-shaped splat and molded back uprights.

CARD TABLE, made in Baltimore, Maryland, is mahogany with eagle inlays.

SETTEE has back painted with peacock feathers; square, tapering legs are painted in a similar motif.

PEMBROKE TABLE is mahogany with decorative inlay.

SIDE CHAIR, one of a set of six, is mahogany; carved shield back displays medallion.

1780 *George Hepplewhite* 1800

Furniture produced after 1780 usually is referred to by names of leading designers. George Hepplewhite, for example, was as much a classicist as Robert Adam, and Hepplewhite's book *The Cabinet-Maker and Upholsterer's Guide*, published posthumously in 1788, showed cabinetmakers how to apply Adam's principles of elegance combined with utility. Nearly three hundred different patterns in the book imply by their curving lines that Hepplewhite absorbed a good deal from Chippendale too. Contributing to a fastidious gracefulness were oval-, shield- and heart-shaped backs on chairs that had square, tapering legs. Arm supports continued from front legs to above the seat and then swept backwards in a pronounced curve to join the back of the chair about halfway up. Carving now was less important than inlay or painting. The sideboard as one unit emerged from the side table flanked by two pedestals that was so general into the 1770's.

Hepplewhite's style dominated the early years (1780–1800) of the Federal furniture period in the United States. Here motifs included classical urns, sheaves of wheat and the eagle.

MIRROR, made in New York, has upper glass panel painted; frame is mahogany and gilt.

ARMCHAIR has a carved oval back displaying Prince of Wales feathers.

WINDOW SEAT has serpentine curve to give it elegance; mahogany frame is carved and inlaid.

CARD TABLE of mahogany has bellflower-and-leaf inlay.

URN STAND is mahogany with fluted legs, scalloped top.

SOFA with the new straight back has frame painted with bellflowers.

SECRETARY of satinwood has cylinder front, oval glass panels in cupboard.

SIDEBOARD with pedestal cupboards is mahogany inlaid with vases and grapes.

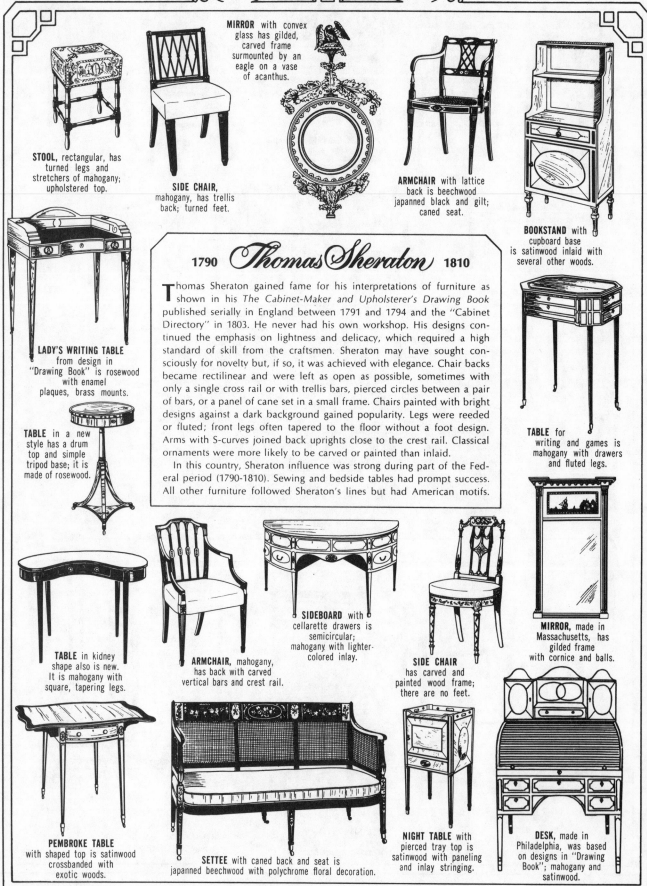

STOOL, rectangular, has turned legs and stretchers of mahogany; upholstered top.

SIDE CHAIR, mahogany, has trellis back; turned feet.

MIRROR with convex glass has gilded, carved frame surmounted by an eagle on a vase of acanthus.

ARMCHAIR with lattice back is beechwood japanned black and gilt; caned seat.

BOOKSTAND with cupboard base is satinwood inlaid with several other woods.

LADY'S WRITING TABLE from design in "Drawing Book" is rosewood with enamel plaques, brass mounts.

TABLE in a new style has a drum top and simple tripod base; it is made of rosewood.

1790 *Thomas Sheraton* 1810

Thomas Sheraton gained fame for his interpretations of furniture as shown in his *The Cabinet-Maker and Upholsterer's Drawing Book* published serially in England between 1791 and 1794 and the "Cabinet Directory" in 1803. He never had his own workshop. His designs continued the emphasis on lightness and delicacy, which required a high standard of skill from the craftsmen. Sheraton may have sought consciously for novelty but, if so, it was achieved with elegance. Chair backs became rectilinear and were left as open as possible, sometimes with only a single cross rail or with trellis bars, pierced circles between a pair of bars, or a panel of cane set in a small frame. Chairs painted with bright designs against a dark background gained popularity. Legs were reeded or fluted; front legs often tapered to the floor without a foot design. Arms with S-curves joined back uprights close to the crest rail. Classical ornaments were more likely to be carved or painted than inlaid.

In this country, Sheraton influence was strong during part of the Federal period (1790-1810). Sewing and bedside tables had prompt success. All other furniture followed Sheraton's lines but had American motifs.

TABLE for writing and games is mahogany with drawers and fluted legs.

MIRROR, made in Massachusetts, has gilded frame with cornice and balls.

TABLE in kidney shape also is new. It is mahogany with square, tapering legs.

ARMCHAIR, mahogany, has back with carved vertical bars and crest rail.

SIDEBOARD with cellarette drawers is semicircular; mahogany with lighter-colored inlay.

SIDE CHAIR has carved and painted wood frame; there are no feet.

PEMBROKE TABLE with shaped top is satinwood crossbanded with exotic woods.

SETTEE with caned back and seat is japanned beechwood with polychrome floral decoration.

NIGHT TABLE with pierced tray top is satinwood with paneling and inlay stringing.

DESK, made in Philadelphia, was based on designs in "Drawing Book"; mahogany and satinwood.

The European
Background

FRENCH

Provincial

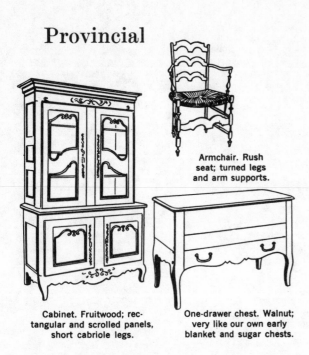

Armchair. Rush seat; turned legs and arm supports.

Cabinet. Fruitwood; rectangular and scrolled panels, short cabriole legs.

One-drawer chest. Walnut; very like our own early blanket and sugar chests.

Louis XIV

Armchair. Silvered frame, turned and carved; cut velvet.

Wardrobe (armoire). Ebony; Boulle-work decoration strikingly set off by the dark wood background.

Candlestand (torchère). Tripod base; gilded.

Writing table (bureau plat). Ebony; Boulle-work decoration; shaped serpentine cross-stretchers; bronze doré mounts. Form continues into nineteenth century.

FRENCH FURNITURE STYLES

FRENCH

The court of Louis XIV was the most magnificent the modern world has known, and the furniture in the LOUIS XIV style (1643-1715) is appropriately grand: massive and symmetrical; carved, gilded, silvered; decorated with marquetry or elaborate tortoise-shell and metal inlay (Boulle work). RÉGENCE (1715-1723) is the term applied to furniture produced during the minority of Louis XV, a period of artistic as well as political transition, when straight lines begin to yield to curves and ornament is increasingly naturalistic. The rococo LOUIS XV style (1723-1774) reflects the growing importance of women at the court. Curves are everywhere; so are appliqués of chased and gilded bronze (*bronze doré*) and incredibly skillful marquetry. (Most of the FRENCH PROVINCIAL so popular today is a simplified version of Louis XV forms.) The ill-fated LOUIS XVI (1774-1793) gave his name to a style in which straight lines are again dominant, with proportions and motifs derived from the classical. Craftsmen trained under the old guilds gave a measure of distinction to the post-Revolutionary DIRECTOIRE style (1795-1804); they discreetly worked the new patriotic emblems into its decoration. Military symbols and Napoleon's personal insignia—bee, crown and letter N—are added in the EMPIRE period (1804-1815), and many of the furniture forms are heavier, with much less ornamentation.

Louis XVI

Love seat. Carved and painted frame; brocade upholstery.

Chest of drawers. Tulipwood, marble top; fluted corner posts; bronze doré applied trim.

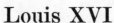

Side chair. Carved and silvered; upholstered in velvet.

Architect's table. Mahogany, leather top; brass trim.

Armchair. Carved walnut covered in tapestry; fluted, tapered legs.

Fall-front secretary. Ebony and lacquer; **bronze doré** trim.

Bouillotte lamp. Named for a popular game.

Writing table. Mahogany; inlaid and mounted in **bronze doré**; fluted, tapered legs.

Régence

Candlestick. Silver; baluster form.

Wardrobe. Paneled, carved and inlaid; **bronze doré** trim.

Console table. Oak; elaborately carved; shaped marble top; line of skirt conforms to top.

Armchair. Beechwood; caned seat and back.

Louis XV

Corner chair. Carved walnut; back and seat upholstered in leather.

Lady's desk. Drawers at back raised by a spring.

Sconce. Two lights; typically rococo in shape; **bronze doré.**

Armchair with open arms (fauteuil). Walnut; covered with tapestry.

Chaise longue. In two parts, armchair and ottoman; carved beechwood frame upholstered in velvet; loose pillow.

Armchair with arms and back in one piece (bergère).

Sofa (canapé). Carved and gilded wood, satin upholstery. Designed to provide the luxurious comfort this period is known for.

Directoire and Empire

Chandelier. Brass and crystal; popular Egyptian motifs.

Armchair. Rosewood; swan-neck arm supports, saber legs.

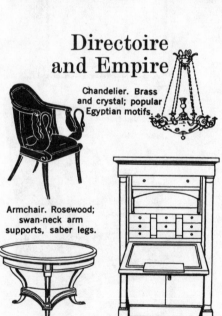

Center table. Mahogany, inlaid with ebony and boxwood; lion-paw feet.

Fall-front secretary. Marble top; gilded bronze column mounts.

Fall-front secretary. Floral and geometric marquetry.

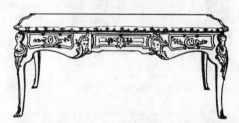

Writing table. Mahogany; masks at corners and ornamental scrollwork, **bronze doré,** concealing handles and lock escutcheons.

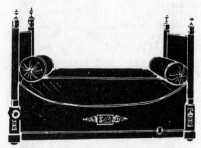

Bed. Rosewood; head and foot of equal height; brass appliqués. Shows bulkiness of form typical of latter part of this period.

Commode. Two drawers; handles and drawer divisions masked by **bronze doré** trim.

Cylinder-top desk. Geometric inlay (parquetry); **bronze doré** handles, feet and mounts.

Woman's Day
DICTIONARY of FRENCH FURNITURE
By DOROTHY H. JENKINS

Furniture ranks among the arts of France as truly as painting and sculpture. For two centuries, under the patronage of luxury-loving monarchs, artisans produced the most decorative furnishings the world has ever seen. The French mode prevailed in the United States from about 1790 until almost 1840; today antique French furniture, particularly that of the eighteenth century, receives appreciation from connoisseurs here and throughout the world. Especially popular in this country are the old French Provincial styles. Beginning with Louis XIII, French furniture falls into periods named for the reigns. Each of these period styles has some characteristics in common with English and American furniture of the same span of years. However, the elegant details of the workmanship give French styles a totally distinctive grace and beauty. The Renaissance attracted architects, painters, sculptors, *ébénistes* (cabinetmakers of quality), *menuisiers* (workers in solid wood rather than veneers) and specialists in other materials to the French court. These artisans contributed to the making of furniture from beautiful woods that were carved magnificently and decorated exquisitely with inlay and marquetry. While elaborate furniture in great quantity was produced for the French court and the homes of noblemen, less luxurious furniture was being made in the provinces. Provincial pieces were much simpler in design and materials, but lines and decoration changed with each period. Wherever it originated, French furniture included familiar pieces. For example, a *torchère* is equivalent to the American candlestand; a *commode* is a chest of drawers; a *régulateur* is a tall case clock or a grandfather clock.

Illustrations by HELEN DISBROW

PROVINCIAL
Louis XIV encoignure (corner cupboard).

PROVINCIAL
Empire console (wall table).

RÉGENCE
Bombé commode (convex chest of drawers).

LOUIS XV
Table en haricot (kidney-shaped table).

PROVINCIAL
Louis XVI glace (mirror), carved frame.

LOUIS XVI
Bergère (chair with closed arms).

DIRECTOIRE
Petit canapé (settee), mahogany frame.

ARMOIRE (clothes cupboard) of ebony with boulle inlay decoration.

CONSOLE (wall table) of carved and gilded wood with a marble top.

MOTIFS popular for decoration were the acanthus leaf, sunburst and mask.

COMMODE (chest of drawers) is walnut with serpentine drawers ornamented by molding.

LOUIS XIV
1643-1715

Louis XIV, who ruled for a long period of great prosperity, built the *Palais de Versailles* where the most magnificent court the world has ever seen was maintained. Grand and massive furniture was built for this era of elegance and splendor. Pieces were made basically in a classic style with rectilinear lines that were well balanced and softened by rich carving, which often was gilded or silvered. Motifs included the classic acanthus leaf and mask, and also a sunburst, the emblem of Louis XIV. Marquetry, veneered inlay in designs with vari-colored woods, was much used and boulle work, inlay of tortoise shell and metal named for furniture maker André Charles Boulle, was introduced. Gilded mounts, either *bronze doré* (gilded bronze) or ormolu (gilded bronze or other metal), were popular.

FAUTEUIL (chair with open arms); caned seat and back.

TABOURET (stool) has top worked in petit point.

BERGÈRE (chair with closed arms) has carved frame; one of a pair.

FAUTEUIL of carved beechwood has cabriole legs.

ENCOIGNURE (corner cupboard) is paneled and decorated with brass inlay.

BUREAU PLAT by Charles Cressent, a student of Boulle.

BUREAU PLAT (writing table) with inlay, probably by Boulle.

TABLE DE MILIEU (center table), carved and gilded; legs in form of fantastic animals.

FAUTEUIL has back and seat upholstered.

BUREAU PLAT has elaborate marquetry on drawer-fronts and legs.

RÉGENCE
1715-1723

The *Régence* years, covering Louis XV's minority, were a period of transition between the classic style of Louis XIV and the lighter-appearing rococo furniture that became the vogue while Louis XV was monarch. Probably no one discarded Louis XIV pieces, but their straight lines gradually were superseded by curving ones in new furniture. Chairs acquired the cabriole leg, which curves out at the knee and in above the foot, instead of a straight leg; backs were lower and gently curved instead of high and rigid. Carvings became more delicate, and were based on such naturalistic motifs as rocks, shells, birds and foliage.

DÉCOR, graceful drawer pull (below, top) and shell, a favorite motif.

FAUTEUIL (chair with open arms) carved with flowers and foliage and caned.

LIT DE REPOS (day bed) with outward-curving scroll ends was a new and comfortable introduction.

FAUTEUIL with carved and painted frame.

TABOURET, one of a pair, carved and gilded.

CHIFFONNIER has a drawer for each day of the week.

LOUIS XV
1723-1774

More new pieces of furniture were introduced during the reign of Louis XV than in any earlier period. One style of chair, called a *marquise*, typified the trend; this was a wide armchair or small sofa built to accommodate the wide skirts and panniers worn by the ladies. All furniture had curving, graceful lines and although decoration continued to be lavish, it was delicate and attractive. Table tops often were marble, and some chairs had caned seats. Wood was more often painted daintily, gilded or silvered than left in its natural color. Lacquered surfaces also became fashionable.

Another new style of chair was the *bergère*, large and deep with closed arms. The *canapé* (sofa), *lit de repos* (day bed), *coiffeuse* (dressing table) and the drop-leaf desk were other introductions. A diversity of game tables, a *liseuse* (reading table) with a collapsible bookrest in the center of the top, and many small tables for various purposes became common.

SECRÉTAIRE EN PENTE (slant-front desk) is small, has drop leaf and serpentine drawer.

BUREAU PLAT has cabriole legs and graceful carving.

CONSOLE, one of a pair, is elaborately carved and gilded.

COMMODE EN TOMBEAUX (chest of drawers with short legs).

SECRÉTAIRE À ABATTANT, (desk with fall front for writing surface); decorated with marquetry.

COMMODE with two drawers has marble top, marquetry decoration.

OTTOMANE (oval-shaped sofa) has incurved arms, gilded wood.

MARQUISE (wide armchair or a small sofa); one of a pair.

CHAISE (side chair) has cabriole legs and carving on crest.

CANAPÉ, more open than ottomane above left, has a carved and gilded frame.

TABLE EN CHIFFONNIER (occasional table) has pull-out writing slide above drawers.

FAUTEUIL DE CABINET (desk chair); rounded.

MARQUISE, one of a pair, with flat back, carved and gilded.

BONHEUR-DU-JOUR (small desk with compartment at back); tambour doors.

SECRÉTAIRE À ABATTANT (fall-front desk), has ceramic plaque in center.

TABLE À TRICTRAC (backgammon table) has reversible top.

FAUTEUIL with fluted legs is carved and gilded.

DECORATIVE MOTIFS: lyre, rosette, reeding.

TABOURET, still important, is painted and gilded.

LOUIS XVI
1774-1792

Before Louis XVI became King of France, a new furniture style was presaged by certain changes. Marquetry patterns tended to be simplified and more geometrical, and curving of furniture parts became gentler and, as the new style became established, straightened out. Straight lines became so dominant that they were emphasized on chair legs by vertical reeding or fluting, and the stiles (outside vertical pieces) on *commodes* had flat cut corners. A revival of interest in classical forms, inspired by the earlier discovery of Herculaneum and Pompeii, made popular such decorative motifs as lyres, urns, wreaths and rosettes. *Acajou* (mahogany) became the favorite wood and often was enriched with bronze. Toward the end of the period, mahogany with wavy grain was used effectively.

Luxurious furniture continued to be made in quantity. Important new pieces were dining tables of solid mahogany with drop leaves, a serving table with marble top and shelves below, and a *bonheur-du-jour* or small writing desk with a little cupboard at the back. Also making its first appearance was the *tricoteuse* or worktable with a pierced metal gallery around the top, one side of which could be lowered. *Guéridons,* or round tables, were made in all sizes from one small enough for a candlestick to those large enough for the card game *bouillotte;* the latter usually were made of mahogany with an openwork brass gallery and perhaps a marble top. Special tables for *trictrac* (backgammon) and other games were made in quantity. These were usually made of mahogany and were rectangular with removable or reversible tops; one side was covered in leather, the other in baize. When the top was in place, the table looked like a flat-topped writing table.

BERGÈRE, one of a pair, carved and gilded.

BUREAU À CYLINDRE (roll-top desk) was handsomely decorated and popular.

TABLE À ÉCRIRE (small writing table) with two drawers, marquetry trim.

CANAPÉ matches *bergère* shown above right.

COMMODE-SERVANTE (sideboard with undershelf), marble top.

BUREAU PLAT is mahogany with gilded-bronze rim.

LIT DE REPOS (day bed) has painted frame.

COMMODE with marble top has inlaid drawers.

CANAPÉ has rectilinear frame of fruitwood.

COMMODE, in a demilune shape, has drawers in front and side cabinets.

TABLE À CAFÉ (serving table) has design of inlay, gilded-bronze gallery.

CHAISE (side chair), painted, has carved lyre back.

TABLE À DÉJEUNER (tea table) has tilt top and gilded-bronze gallery; mahogany.

CONSOLE is carved, painted and gilded; marble top.

DIRECTOIRE
1795-1804

This first of two periods when Napoleon Bonaparte was pre-eminent in France is distinguished by striking changes in the decoration of furniture rather than in its over-all design. The classical influence was still strong, but the griffins, sphinxes, swans and fasces chosen for ornament reflected Napoleon's campaigns in Italy and Egypt. The tripod or pedestal base on tables became general. More solid mahogany was used and marquetry was seen less and less. Mahogany became the chief wood and, after 1799, lemon-wood became popular for the contrast of its light color. Chairs were made with saber legs: front legs curved forward, rear legs backward. The legs often terminated in lion's-paw feet of brass. Backs on chairs often had an outward curve, and backs on *canapés* were scrolled. New pieces of furniture included the *méridienne*, a type of short sofa; the cheval glass, a full-length mirror framed and mounted on a wooden support so it could be tilted, and the bed, in the form of a sleigh, with the headboard and footboard the same height.

COMMODE, mahogany, has rich marquetry, marble top.

VITRINE (display cabinet) has adjustable glass shelves.

CHAUFFE-ASSIETTES (plate-warmer) is brass and tole.

MOTIFS: rosette (left) and griffin.

BERGÈRE has ormolu mounts.

ATHÉNIENNE (stand for a plant or candle).

CHAISE (side chair) has saber legs, outcurved back.

CHAISE, shaped and carved back; saber legs.

TABLE DE MILIEU (center table) on tripod base is walnut, partly painted.

TABLE À ÉCRIRE (small writing desk) has color print framed in gilded copper on top.

PETIT CANAPÉ (settee) with lyre back has typical striped upholstery.

FAUTEUIL DE CABINET (desk chair); ormolu mounts.

GUÉRIDON (candlestand); griffin-carved legs.

FAUTEUIL has carved swan-neck arm supports.

CHAISE has curved and classically carved back.

COMMODE of mahogany has columns at front corners.

MOTIFS: sphinx, lion's-paw foot.

EMPIRE
1804-1814

The decade during which Napoleon was Emperor established a style of furniture that became known as Empire. Its influence was far-reaching and, in the United States, continued until almost 1840. Contributing to the massiveness of various pieces was dark mahogany, which often was embellished with elaborate gilded bronzes. Lines were chiefly rectilinear and sometimes were set off by columns of bronze, marble or wood. In addition to sphinxes, winged lions, eagles and swans, other decorative motifs were based on Napoleon's personal insignia: the bee, a crown or the initial "N."

PROVINCIAL

FAUTEUIL, Louis XIV, has "X" stretchers; minimum carving.

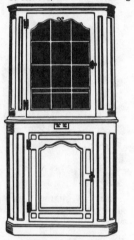

ENCOIGNURE, circa 1800, is in two parts; glazed doors.

ARMOIRE, Louis XV, is tall, has doors in two parts.

Provincial is the term for furniture made in the provinces of France during the various periods of the seventeenth and eighteenth centuries. All of this extensive group is less sophisticated and less heavily decorated than furniture produced in Paris and for members of the court. The making of Provincial pieces began during Louis XIV's reign when court furniture became so varied and luxurious. The basic furniture for a French home always has been the *armoire* (clothes cupboard), table, bed and chair. *Tabourets* (stools) continued to be popular long after chairs were common. However, new pieces were copied by Provincial cabinetmakers as soon as they heard about them, so not only tables and chairs but furniture in general became more varied. Lines of traditional pieces changed from period to period too. Thus Provincial furniture made during the Louis XIV period was carved, but was not as heavily carved or as massive as that made in Paris. During the days of Louis XV, Provincial furniture could be described as simplified rococo with curving lines, but in the provinces, as at court, the curving lines changed to straight ones during the reign of Louis XVI and Marie Antoinette.

A few of the Provincial cabinetmakers, in Grenoble and Dijon and other centers, turned out such elegantly simple pieces that their names are still known. Antique Provincial furniture varies in quality according to the skill of the man who made it. As with American country furniture, French Provincial was made not only by cabinetmakers but also by carpenters. These less skilled woodworkers often turned out pieces that were almost crude and lacked good proportions. Provincial furniture makers worked with woods of the region in which they lived. A great deal of oak was used and this wood ages to a mellow beauty. Chestnut, with a grain that somewhat resembles oak, and walnut were other favorites; beech and ash were chosen for contrast. And, of course, the fruitwoods, cherry and the lighter-colored pearwood and applewood, were especially well liked. Brown was the dominant color but the various common woods ranged from a very light tint to almost black. *Acajou* (mahogany), which was imported, was used to some extent during the Louis XVI period. Provincial furniture frequently was painted a soft gray, green or blue. Upholstery fabrics were quite likely to be gay with naturalistic flowers. Chairs often had rush seats and among French Provincial ones are to be found some counterparts of American furniture: for example, the ladder-back chair with comparatively short legs and a rush seat.

CONFORTABLE (wing chair), Louis XV, has more upholstery than wood.

ARMOIRE, Louis XV, is oak with rococo carving on the doors.

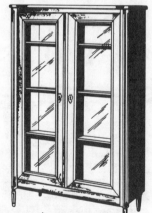

BIBLIOTHÈQUE (bookcase), Louis XVI, is fruitwood fitted with shelves and glass doors.

COMMODE-SECRÉTAIRE (slant-front desk), Louis XV, is walnut with paneled drawers.

CONSOLE, Louis XV, has shell carving, cabriole legs.

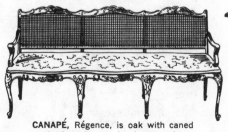

CANAPÉ, Régence, is oak with caned back and seat plus loose pad.

TABLE À OUVRAGE (worktable), Louis XVI.

BERGÈRE, Louis XVI, has simple frame and flowered upholstery.

LIT (bed), Louis XV, has curving lines carved in fruitwood.

SECRÉTAIRE À ABATTANT, late 1700's, is fruitwood, has bureau front.

TABOURET, Louis XVI, was always popular.

FAUTEUIL DE CABINET, Louis XV.

LIT, Louis XVI, is curved less and painted.

BUREAU PLAT, Louis XV, is three drawers wide.

FAUTEUIL, Louis XV, is plainly upholstered.

CHAISE, Louis XV, has caned seat and back.

COMMODE, Louis XVI, is mahogany with marble top.

FAUTEUIL, Louis XV, beechwood; rush seat.

CHAISE, Louis XVI, has straight lines.

PETIT CANAPÉ, Directoire, is mahogany, with modified lyre back, loose cushion.

TABLE EN CHIFFONNIER (occasional table), Louis XV.

TABLE DE SALLE À MANGER (dining table), Louis XVI, has drop leaves.

TABLE DE NUIT (bedside table), Louis XVI.

COMMODE À ENCOIGNURES (rounded chest of drawers), Louis XVI.

OTTOMANE (oval-shaped sofa), Louis XVI; walnut frame.

COMMODE À VANTAUX (chest with doors), Louis XV; oak with surface carving.

MÉRIDIENNE, Empire, has outcurved arms and legs; one arm higher than other.

BIBLIOTHÈQUE-SECRÉTAIRE À ABATTANT, Louis XVI, is mahogany, has bookshelves and fall front.

TABLE DE JEU (game table), Louis XV.

CHAISE, Louis XV, is beechwood; rush seat, ladder back.

BRAS DE LUMIÈRE (sconce), Louis XV; gilded bronze, three branches.

CANDÉLABRE (candelabrum), Empire.

LAMPE BOUILLOTTE (game-table lamp), Louis XVI.

LUSTRE (chandelier), Louis XVI; crystal and ormolu.

BRAS DE LUMIÈRE Louis XVI; gilded bronze.

CARTEL (hanging wall clock), Louis XV.

GLACE (mirror), Provincial Louis XVI; carved and painted.

CHENETS (andirons), Louis XV; gilded bronze.

TRUMEAU (mirror with painting at top), Provincial Louis XV.

GLACE, Louis XV, carved and gilded.

Accessories & Bibelots

Almost as important as the furniture in a room were the accessories of gold, silver and bronze, tortoise shell, enamel, faïence and porcelain, lacquer, crystal and wood, the latter intricately carved or inlaid. Styles in accessories changed with each furniture period. In spite of all the luxury, illumination after dark was poor. Candlesticks and *bras de lumière* (wall sconces) in pairs were handsome but gave comparatively little light; however, in the eighteenth century chandeliers became common. The mantel shelf that appeared over fireplaces in the seventeenth century provided a place for a candelabrum flanked by single candlesticks. Mirrors were enhanced by magnificently wrought frames. Both *régulateurs* (tall case clocks) and wall clocks were first made during the seventeenth century. Snuffboxes, inkstands and vases were frequently works of art.

CHANDELIERS (candlesticks), Louis XV; gilded bronze.

GLACE, Directoire.

PENDULE (clock), Provincial; lyre form.

PSYCHÉ (cheval glass), Empire, ormolu mounts.

BAROMÈTRE (barometer), Louis XVI; gilded bronze, steel face.

RÉGULATEUR (tall case clock), Louis XIV.

PENDULE, Louis XVI; gilded bronze and statuary marble.

CHANDELIER (candlestick), Louis XVI; two-toned bronze.

ENCRIER (inkstand), Louis XVI.

GLACE, Provincial Empire, is hung over a mantel.

American Classics

PILGRIM AND WILLIAM AND MARY

QUEEN ANNE AND CHIPPENDALE

FEDERAL

Pilgrim

Guilford chest. Pine, with painted decoration originally black, gay reds, yellows.

Connecticut two-drawer chest. Sunflower and tulip carving, ebonized bosses and split spindles.

Press cupboard. Raised panels, saw-tooth decoration, bulb-turned supports, bun feet.

Court cupboard. Split spindles, vase-turned supports, ball feet; open space for display of plates.

Bible or writing box. Simple geometric chisel carving, molded edges.

Accessories: brass candlestick brought from England; wooden cup made here.

Spice cupboard. Sunken molded panel, split spindles; old red paint.

Joint stool. Oak; baluster-turned legs, box stretcher. Commonest early form of seat.

AMERICAN FURNITURE STYLES

PILGRIM and WILLIAM and MARY

No matter how many pieces of furniture are supposed to have come over in the *Mayflower*, the earliest settlers in America cannot have brought much with them. They had to make what they needed, using mostly oak and pine and following familiar English styles: Tudor, Jacobean, Restoration. Elements of all these are present, though necessarily simplified, in PILGRIM (1620-1690) furniture. Turning (parts shaped on a lathe) is the characteristic decoration; applied turned trim is often painted black to look like expensive ebony. By the end of the seventeenth century things were easier for the colonists and they could pay more attention to the niceties of living. In the WILLIAM AND MARY style (1690-1725) we find greater variety of forms, new woods, notably walnut, and new types of decoration. Turning is still important, but caning and japanning appear, and there are more upholstered pieces. "Survival" pieces (simplified versions made in outlying areas long after the forms are out of fashion) exist in these styles and in later ones as well.

William and Mary

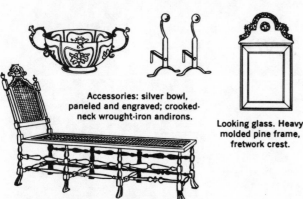

Accessories: silver bowl, paneled and engraved; crooked-neck wrought-iron andirons.

Looking glass. Heavy molded pine frame, fretwork crest.

Double-stretcher day bed. Flemish scroll crest, cane seat and back, block-and-turned legs and stretchers, sharply canted back.

Butterfly drop-leaf table. Maple; canted legs, conforming drawer.

Tea table. Arched, scalloped skirt, simple turning, molded edge.

Gate-leg table. Walnut; eight baluster-turned legs, two gates, Spanish feet.

Lowboy. Walnut; shaped skirt, acorn drops, serpentine cross-stretcher.

Three-legged spindle chair. Triangular seat and stretcher.

Child's chair. Maple and elm; simple turnings.

Brewster armchair. Spindles, heavy turned posts; wood seat.

Cromwellian side chair. Maple; sausage turnings.

Wainscot armchair. Paneled frame, square posts.

Table chair. Chestnut; box seat, turned arms, legs and stretchers.

Desk-on-chest-on-frame. Block-and-turned legs.

One-drawer chest-on-frame. Applied bosses, sausage-turned stretchers.

Gate-leg table with drawer. Eight legs, four gates, ball-and-ring turned legs and stretchers.

Trestle table. Oak frame, maple top cut from one board. Form persists well into nineteenth century in remote country districts.

Wing chair. Sharply scrolled arms; separate cushion (squab).

Banister back chair. Maple; rush seat.

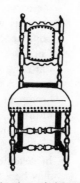
Leather-upholstered chair. Walnut; painted black.

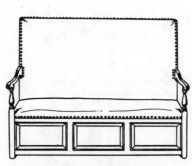
Settle. Walnut and black leather; box seat, paneled, conceals chest. Some settles convert into beds.

Slant-front desk-on-chest. Maple and walnut; arched tops on pigeonholes.

Japanned highboy. Black lacquer and gilt; six trumpet-turned legs, bail handles.

Chest-on-frame. Plain flat molded top, five legs, S-curved stretcher, turnip feet.

Fall-front desk-on-chest. Heavy molding at top; teardrop handles.

Hudson Valley wardrobe (kas). Oak and gumwood; flaring cornice, elaborate paneling, single drawer in base.

Queen Anne **Chippendale**

Easy chairs. Cabriole leg (shaped like a bent knee), with or without simple carving, starts with Queen Anne; Chippendale version more elaborately carved.

Side chairs. Stretchers, flat and shaped or turned, occur sometimes on Queen Anne chairs, have disappeared by Chippendale period. Back legs on both slightly canted.

Armchairs. Queen Anne has hoop-shaped back; most commonly found Chippendale back is rectangular with Cupid's-bow crest rail. Both may have shell carving.

Corner chairs. A new form. Queen Anne splat is solid, vase-shaped; Chippendale splats are pierced in a wide variety of designs. Slip seats on both. Turned arm supports.

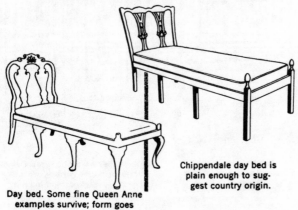

Day bed. Some fine Queen Anne examples survive; form goes out of fashion in this period.

Chippendale day bed is plain enough to suggest country origin.

Queen Anne **Chippendale**

Looking glasses. Frames show increased elegance of Chippendale style with phoenix finial.

Tall-case (grandfather) clocks. Shape changes little throughout eighteenth century; differences appear in decorative details: panel shape, inlay, bonnet, finials.

AMERICAN FURNITURE STYLES, *continued*

QUEEN ANNE *and* CHIPPENDALE

The QUEEN ANNE style (1725-1750) brought to American furniture greater lightness and grace and a new concept of comfort: chairs shaped to fit the body, and new forms introduced to meet the needs of an increasingly urbane way of life. The most fashionable wood is walnut, though cherry and maple are also popular. Mahogany becomes important about 1750. Carving is the principal embellishment. In the CHIPPENDALE period (1750-1775) the elements of the Queen Anne style are kept but a good deal of rococo ornamentation is added. American Chippendale furniture of the great centers, Philadelphia, Newport, Boston and New York, compares favorably with the best efforts of the contemporary English craftsmen. In seventeenth- and eighteenth-century styles there may be a time lag of ten to twenty years between the development of the new in Europe and its adoption here. This lag decreases as communications improve. Transition pieces, retaining features of earlier styles or adding new ones to old forms, are always found.

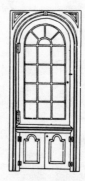 

Corner cupboards. Built-in or movable (made in two parts). Pitch pediment replacing arch at top is Chippendale innovation; bracket feet at right.

Queen Anne   Chippendale

Lowboys. Finest surviving examples are in elaborately carved Chippendale style. Claw-and-ball foot has replaced earlier pad, drake (three-lobed) or slipper foot (left).

Desks. Desk-on-frame has shaped skirt; form goes out with Queen Anne. Block-front desk-on-chest is major New England Chippendale contribution; butterfly brasses.

Highboys. Often made to match lowboys. Flat top goes out of style early; bonnet top at right seen also on Queen Anne pieces; flame finials, fluted corner columns.

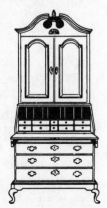

Secretaries. Simple arch paneling (left) reflects differences in style. Bombé or kettle base on right is found only on Chippendale chests, desks and secretaries.

Queen Anne   Chippendale

Tray-top tables. Narrow carved ornament on skirt of Chippendale example (seen also on Chippendale card table below) is called gadrooning.

Tilt-top tables. As popular on first appearance as they are today, for the same reason: they save space. Piecrust edge on table at right.

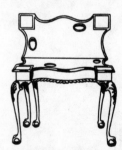

Card tables. Queen Anne has rare needlework top; both have oval saucers for counters and space at corners for candlesticks. Chippendale has extra leg.

Marble-top tables. Used in dining room before the sideboard was developed, for same purpose. Drake foot on Queen Anne, French scrolled toe on Chippendale.

Drop-leaf tables. Oval, round or rectangular, popular in both periods for dining. Chippendale drop-leafs may have six or eight legs; Queen Anne, at left, uses one of four legs as gate.

CHINA CABINET, mahogany with fretwork, reflects the influence of Chinese design.

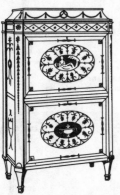

ARMCHAIR, one of a set of six, is carved mahogany with tapestry covering.

SECRETAIRE, or small bureau desk, is satinwood fancifully inlaid.

COMMODE with fretwork gallery is japanned in black and gold.

American Chippendale
1755-1780

Thomas Chippendale revolutionized furniture fashion in America. Here as in England, skillful cabinetmakers executed splendid carving, well-proportioned cabriole legs, and the various forms of chair backs inspired by Chippendale. They worked chiefly with mahogany, but also with cherry, maple and walnut. Still, a distinctly American version of Chippendale's style evolved here. Most typically American are bureaus, desks and other case pieces with block fronts; some of these, notably examples made in Newport, Rhode Island, have each blocked panel crowned with a superbly carved shell. The scrolled bonnet-top pediment was used more here to add grace to tall chest-on-chests, highboys and secretaries. On the other hand, galleries were more common on small tables in England than in America.

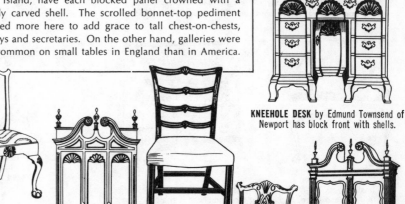

SIDE CHAIR, made in Philadelphia, has carved scroll splat, shell in crest.

SIDE CHAIR has ladder back in an original Philadelphia design.

BUREAU, mahogany, has block front of three vertical panels, center one receding.

KNEEHOLE DESK by Edmund Townsend of Newport has block front with shells.

SECRETARY is fully blocked with carved shells above vertical panels.

SIDE CHAIR, also from Philadelphia, has splat with tassel.

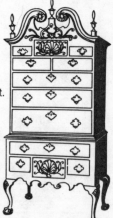

SECRETARY, made in New England, is mahogany with bombé or kettle base.

SIDE CHAIR, mahogany, made in Philadelphia, has lacy scrolled splat.

MIRROR has mahogany frame with gilded side draperies, foliage and bird.

BUREAU, mahogany, with block front and shells, came from Newport.

PEMBROKE TABLE, new, has narrow drop leaves, broad fixed leaf and drawer beneath.

CHEST-ON-CHEST, New England, has willow mounts, carved shell, and bonnet top.

HIGHBOY, walnut, has richly carved broken-arch top; cabriole legs, and shells.

WASHSTAND
in the Hepplewhite manner.

BANJO CLOCK
by Simon Willard, Roxbury.

BEDSIDE TABLE
by John Seymour, Boston.

WOMAN'S DAY DICTIONARY OF
AMERICAN
FEDERAL FURNITURE

By DOROTHY H. JENKINS

★ ★ ★ ★

The manner in which Americans began to furnish their homes in the decade after the Revolutionary War reflected their pride in their new and growing nation. As a result, the words "Federal Period" now refer to the furniture and decorative pieces that were made during the years when the United States was establishing and first living under a Federal Government. The eagle dominant in the Great Seal, which was adopted by Congress in 1782, was carved in wood, painted and etched on glass, painted on pottery, printed on paper and stitched into needlework. The eagle was the most popular decorative motif of the Federal years, which are generally given as 1790-1815, but which actually started in the 1780's. Other names for this span are Classic, Neoclassic and Greek Revival because other decorations and forms stemmed from interest in the discovery of Herculaneum and Pompeii earlier in the eighteenth century. The lyre, acanthus leaf, urn and drapery, all true classical motifs, probably were seen first in the books of furniture designs by George Hepplewhite which were brought to America from England in the early 1780's. While these motifs were used widely in the United States, the eagle Americanized the classical revival here. Prosperous cities along the East Coast set the pace in adapting first Hepplewhite, later Sheraton's new designs. By 1800 French fashions emphasizing the classical motifs with gilding and brass mounts became influential here, which was not surprising since the French had been active supporters of the American Revolution. Mahogany was the first choice of woods for elegant Federal furniture. Bureaus helped to replace the familiar highboys, lowboys, and chests-on-chests. Now for the first time, homeowners could have long dining tables and sideboards. Fall-front and tambour desks and a wealth of tables, large and small, for various purposes were made everywhere. All in all, the Federal years marked a period not only of new beginnings but also of prosperity and comparative luxury.

Illustrations by HELEN DISBROW

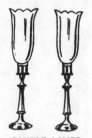

CANDLE LAMPS
Sheffield plate; glass shades.

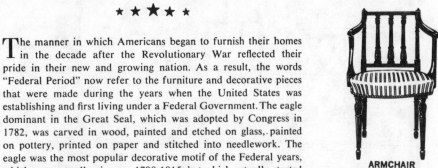

ARMCHAIR
New York City Sheraton.

CANDLESTAND
tilt top, Sheraton style.

CANDELABRUM
brass with painted tin shade,
made in Philadelphia 1804-1814.

SIDE CHAIR
by Duncan Phyfe with lyre
back, carved front legs.

SEWING TABLE
octagonal, carved pedestal;
New York City Sheraton.

GIRANDOLE
with eagle pediment;
candleholders at base.

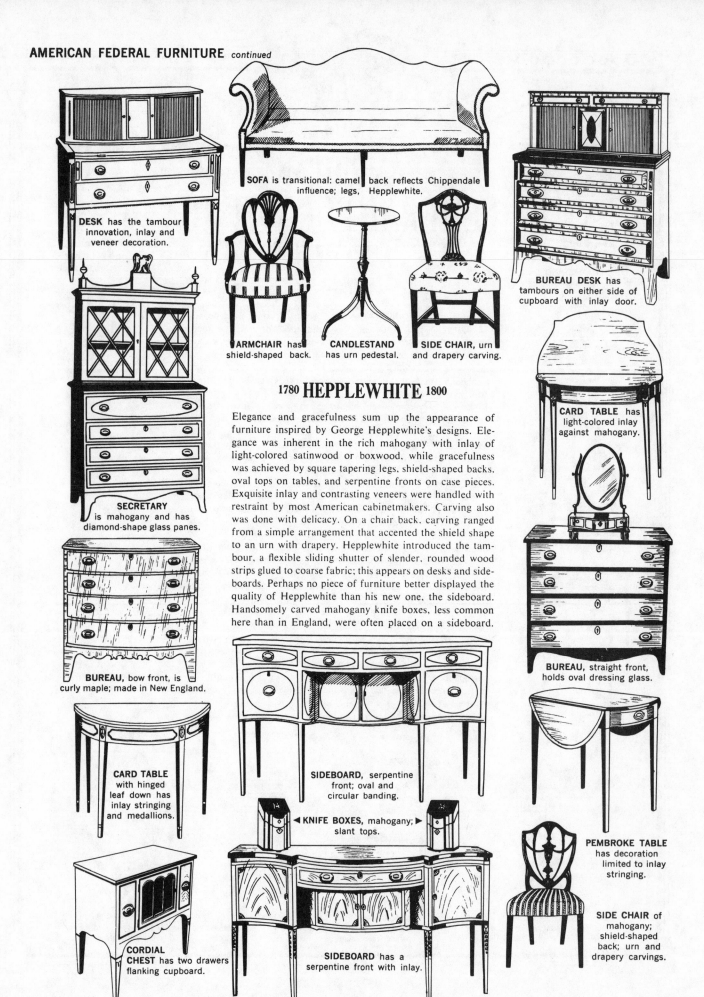

DESK has the tambour innovation, inlay and veneer decoration.

SOFA is transitional: camel back reflects Chippendale influence; legs, Hepplewhite.

ARMCHAIR has shield-shaped back.

CANDLESTAND has urn pedestal.

SIDE CHAIR, urn and drapery carving.

BUREAU DESK has tambours on either side of cupboard with inlay door.

SECRETARY is mahogany and has diamond-shape glass panes.

1780 HEPPLEWHITE 1800

Elegance and gracefulness sum up the appearance of furniture inspired by George Hepplewhite's designs. Elegance was inherent in the rich mahogany with inlay of light-colored satinwood or boxwood, while gracefulness was achieved by square tapering legs, shield-shaped backs, oval tops on tables, and serpentine fronts on case pieces. Exquisite inlay and contrasting veneers were handled with restraint by most American cabinetmakers. Carving also was done with delicacy. On a chair back, carving ranged from a simple arrangement that accented the shield shape to an urn with drapery. Hepplewhite introduced the tambour, a flexible sliding shutter of slender, rounded wood strips glued to coarse fabric; this appears on desks and sideboards. Perhaps no piece of furniture better displayed the quality of Hepplewhite than his new one, the sideboard. Handsomely carved mahogany knife boxes, less common here than in England, were often placed on a sideboard.

CARD TABLE has light-colored inlay against mahogany.

BUREAU, bow front, is curly maple; made in New England.

BUREAU, straight front, holds oval dressing glass.

CARD TABLE with hinged leaf down has inlay stringing and medallions.

SIDEBOARD, serpentine front; oval and circular banding.

◄ **KNIFE BOXES,** mahogany; ► slant tops.

PEMBROKE TABLE has decoration limited to inlay stringing.

SIDE CHAIR of mahogany; shield-shaped back; urn and drapery carvings.

CORDIAL CHEST has two drawers flanking cupboard.

SIDEBOARD has a serpentine front with inlay.

SECRETARY in the Sheraton style is mahogany; has turned and reeded legs; three brass finials.

BREAKFRONT CABINET with glass doors is mahogany and grained mahogany veneer.

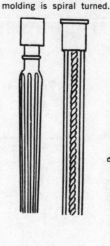

DECORATIONS: Leg (left) is turned and reeded; molding is spiral turned.

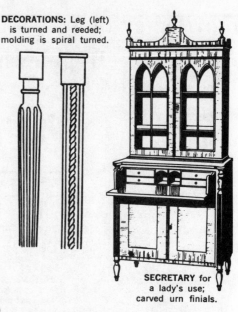

SECRETARY for a lady's use; carved urn finials.

1790 **SHERATON** 1810

Furniture became more diversified yet retained its classical look through the influence of another Englishman, Thomas Sheraton, starting in the 1790's. His designs were graceful although they were based on rectilinear shapes instead of Hepplewhite's oval. The change was most noticeable in chair backs and tables, and was emphasized by vertical reeding of upright members. Inlay became less important, carving more so. Pedestals of tables, for example, often were carved to a lyre or vase shape. Of the many new small tables, none was in greater demand than the one for sewing, and several different types appeared. Sheraton offered his own interpretations of the sideboard and other new pieces introduced by Hepplewhite, and to Sheraton belongs credit for the chest of drawers or bureau with attached mirror. American cabinetmakers often incorporated details of both Sheraton and Hepplewhite in a single piece of furniture.

SIDE CHAIR, mahogany; carved square back; upholstered seat.

BEDSIDE TABLE, mahogany and satinwood, has scalloped shelf.

SEWING TABLE has top that can be raised.

SOFA is 9' long but has excellent proportions.

SIDE CHAIR has carved slat and paw feet on the front legs.

CARD TABLE is mahogany with inlaid bands of satinwood; reeded legs.

SERVING TABLE made of mahogany and satinwood; reeded legs.

SIDE CHAIR; saber legs; eagle carved on center slat.

SIDEBOARD has outcurved corners over reeded posts; legs turned and reeded.

ARMCHAIR has carved splat; reeded legs and spade feet.

SOFA has maghogany frame with cornucopia and wheat sheaves carved along back; front legs are reeded.

DICTIONARY OF FURNITURE

Hepplewhite

Sheraton

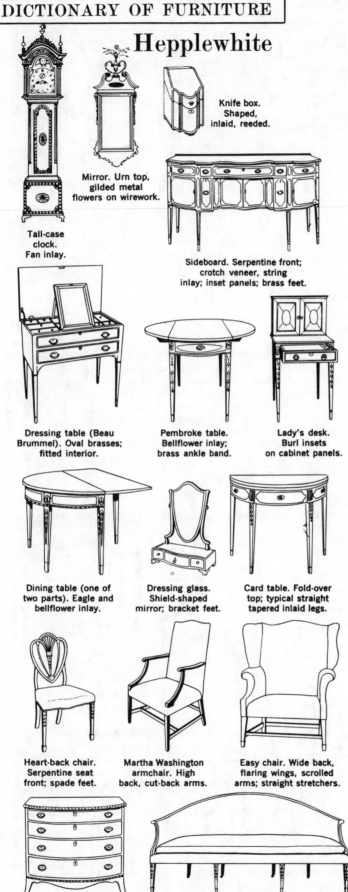

Knife box. Shaped, inlaid, reeded.

Mirror. Urn top, gilded metal flowers on wirework.

Tall-case clock. Fan inlay.

Sideboard. Serpentine front; crotch veneer, string inlay; inset panels; brass feet.

Dressing table (Beau Brummel). Oval brasses; fitted interior.

Pembroke table. Bellflower inlay; brass ankle band.

Lady's desk. Burl insets on cabinet panels.

Dining table (one of two parts). Eagle and bellflower inlay.

Dressing glass. Shield-shaped mirror; bracket feet.

Card table. Fold-over top; typical straight tapered inlaid legs.

Heart-back chair. Serpentine seat front; spade feet.

Martha Washington armchair. High back, cut-back arms.

Easy chair. Wide back, flaring wings, scrolled arms; straight stretchers.

Bow-front chest. Checkered inlaid banding; flaring bracket feet.

Sofa. Continuous-bow back and arms; rear legs square and canted, front legs tapered, inlaid; fluted arm supports.

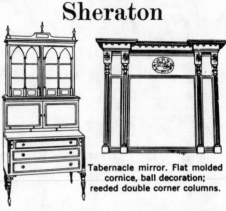

Tabernacle mirror. Flat molded cornice, ball decoration; reeded double corner columns.

Secretary-bookcase. Gothic-arch doors; urn finials.

Sideboard. Mahogany; straight front; carved, fluted, paneled; ring handles hanging from lion heads.

Banjo clock. Painted glass; brass trim.

Chest of drawers. Bow front; reeded and ring-turned corner posts.

Corner washstand. Shaped back and skirt.

Card table. Serpentine skirt and top; inlaid corner blocks.

Worktable. Sewing bag of pleated silk; turned legs, casters.

Sofa. Maple back rail with inlaid medallion; front legs and arm supports vase-shaped and reeded; straight back legs.

FEDERAL

The intensely national atmosphere of the young Republic in the years immediately following the Revolution found expression in the FEDERAL style. This is the period of classicism and of the eagle, carved, painted or inlaid, on furniture made of mahogany, maple, cherry, satinwood. The style has three subdivisions which overlap a good deal. HEPPLEWHITE (1785-1795) introduces graceful, flowing lines, the free-floating chair back, straight tapered legs, serpentine or bowed case pieces. Straight lines come back in the SHERATON style (1790-1810), and turning is important again. Hepplewhite and Sheraton pieces, like their English counterparts, appear elegantly fragile. With DUNCAN PHYFE (1800-1815) there is a return to solidity, a revival of the scrolled line, a new use of metal mounts. Phyfe was the best and most prolific of many American cabinetmakers who worked in the style called by his name, a style based on the Sheraton but also influenced by English Regency and French Directoire. As a matter of fact, very little of the furniture bearing the names of the great cabinetmakers was actually made by them; their fame is based on designs which they produced and which were used by others. Chippendale, oddly enough, is believed to have done his best work in the Adam style while he was working for Robert Adam. Even the label of a particular cabinetmaker means only that the piece bearing it came from his shop: some, notably Phyfe himself, are known to have employed as many as a hundred workmen.

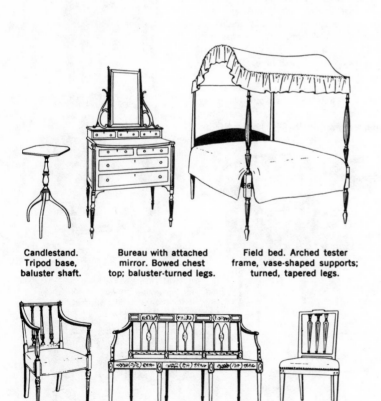

Candlestand. Tripod base, baluster shaft.

Bureau with attached mirror. Bowed chest top; baluster-turned legs.

Field bed. Arched tester frame, vase-shaped supports; turned, tapered legs.

Armchair. Columnar back, pierced splats.

Settee. Painted black and gilt, floral motif; narrow Gothic arch in splats; caned seat.

Side chair. Crested back, pierced splats.

Duncan Phyfe

Convex mirror. Carved, gilded pine frame with spread eagle.

Sofa table. Drop leaves with curved bracket supports; spiral reeding, paw feet.

Side chair. Outcurved lyre-splat back; saber-curved legs.

Armchair. Cane seat; waterleaf carving, dog's-paw front feet.

"Grecian" armchair. Broad, flat crest rail; scrolled arms.

Pier table. Gilt mounts on skirt; legs turned, tapered and reeded.

Card table. Spread-eagle support, four leaf-carved legs.

Window seat. Sides outscrolled; carved rosettes on arms; paw feet and casters of brass.

Worktable. Acorn drops; tripod base.

Sofa. Double-lyre outscrolled arms. Plain crest rail, reeded seat rail; reeded and cornucopia-shaped legs. An extremely popular form.

CARD TABLE has hinged and pivoted octagon top; lyre pedestal on acanthus-carved legs.

CARD TABLE, one of a pair, is distinguished by fine acanthus carving on columns and legs.

MOTIF: Lyre was a great favorite for carving; strings were often brass.

SIDE CHAIR of mahogany has lyre back and carving on front legs; upholstered seat.

SIDE CHAIR with curved seat has reeded legs, drapery-carved crest.

SETTEE with flowing lines has a reeded mahogany frame which is upholstered.

SOFA TABLE, rare, has urn-shaped supports, acanthus carving.

DINING TABLE can be extended from 25" to 13'; columns and egs display acanthus-leaf carving.

1792 DUNCAN PHYFE 1815

One of the great names in the history of American furniture, Duncan Phyfe, is often erroneously considered a synonym for the Federal Period. This cabinetmaker, who opened his shop in New York City in 1792, was perhaps more creative than many of his contemporaries, but there were others fully as skilled. Furthermore, while Phyfe's finest work was done during the Federal Period, he continued to produce furniture of lesser distinction until 1847. His Federal pieces display good proportions, beautiful curving lines, and the high quality of mahogany on which he insisted. He rarely used inlay of lighter woods, but he obtained magnificent effects by inlaying a panel of grained mahogany against plainer mahogany. For the first time, French influence becomes evident in Duncan Phyfe's chairs with saber legs and curving backs, sofas with scrolled lines, classic motifs such as lyre and acanthus, and handsome brass mounts on every possible piece. Clever mechanical devices that made card tables and dining tables easier to use or expand were another facet of Phyfe's creative ability.

SEWING TABLE is octagonal and has a tambour front.

ARMCHAIR of mahogany has delicately carved back, reeded legs, brass paw feet.

BREAKFAST TABLE has a cluster-column support with acanthus-leaf carving.

WORK TABLE with tambour front, hinged top, and writing board; sometimes used for sewing.

LIBRARY TABLE with drop leaves rests on carved urn pedestal; legs have brass paw feet.

WRITING TABLE has hinged lid over hemispherical wells flanking center drawer; trestle support.

PEMBROKE TABLE has unusual serpentine drop leaves; slender reeded legs terminate in brass casters.

COUCH in "Récamier" style has one scrolled end higher than the other; richly carved frame.

SERVER, or small sideboard, has drawers and cupboards that follow the Sheraton lines.

WHATNOT has Canterbury (section for music or loose papers) and one drawer. Sheraton, circa 1810.

ARMCHAIR, one of a pair in a dining-room set. Sheraton, 1810-1815.

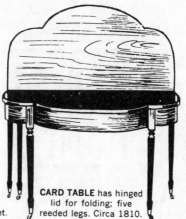

CARD TABLE has hinged lid for folding; five reeded legs. Circa 1810.

SIDE CHAIR, shield back, urn and drapery carving. 1780's.

PEMBROKE TABLE, inlay. Hepplewhite, 1780's.

SEWING TABLE has hinged top for end compartments. 1800-1810.

WORK TABLE by Lannuier has writing board ready for correspondence.

ARMCHAIR, mahogany frame. Hepplewhite, 1780's.

1780 NEW YORK CITY 1815

Fine furniture was available to the rapidly growing city of New York during the Federal Period, and some of it was shipped to cities in states as far away as South Carolina. By no means all of this furniture originated with Duncan Phyfe. During the 1780's and 1790's, many good cabinetmakers were turning out handsome pieces in the Hepplewhite manner. Elbert Anderson (1789-1796) and Mills & Deming (1793-1798) produced tables and sideboards with handsome inlay decoration, and from every cabinetmaker came chairs with carved, shield-shaped backs.

Probably it took Charles-Honoré Lannuier no longer to attract a discriminating clientele when he came to New York in 1805 than it had Duncan Phyfe a decade earlier. Lannuier, a Frenchman, naturally embellished the furniture he made in the United States with typically French details. Like Phyfe, Lannuier preferred to work with mahogany and chose much that was richly grained. He also relied on veneers. Brass was used lavishly for paw feet, decorative medallions, stars and capitals of columns. His carved figures, whether caryatids or eagles, usually were gilded. In addition to sofas, beds, consoles and other tables with a decidedly French look, the versatile Lannuier also successfully adapted the Sheraton style to his own furniture. Sheraton lines and motifs dominated the work of other cabinetmakers in New York City after 1800. The quality of the furniture produced by Michael Allison, George Woodruff and John Dolan, among others, compared most favorably to that of Phyfe and Lannuier.

CARD TABLE by Elbert Anderson displays lines and details of Hepplewhite.

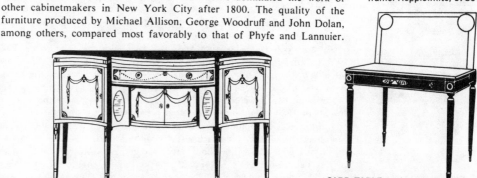

SIDEBOARD by Mills & Deming has serpentine front with exceptional inlay framed with stringing.

CARD TABLE by Lannuier has Sheraton lines, gilded mounts in French style.

CONSOLE TABLE by Lannuier has gilded caryatid supports and dolphin feet.

CARD TABLE by John Hewitt has leaf folded; Hepplewhite in origin.

SOFA TABLE by Lannuier is mahogany with parts of its elaborate carving gilded. Eagle dominates the support.

CARD TABLE of mahogany with bellflower and medallion inlay. Baltimore.

SIDE CHAIR, Sheraton style. Philadelphia, circa 1800.

SIDE CHAIR, bellflower inlay. Baltimore.

SIDEBOARD of mahogany; bellflower inlay on legs; eagles and other designs on front. Baltimore.

SECRETARY is notable for glass doors with drapery-carved frame; broken arch top. Baltimore.

SIDEBOARD, serpentine front, has inlay of the long bellflowers typical of Maryland craftsmen.

SOFA made in Baltimore is upholstered and, more unusual, has bellflower carvings on legs. ▶

PEMBROKE TABLE has oval leaves with inlay stringing. Baltimore.

CARD TABLE has typical Philadelphia carving.

1790 MARYLAND & PHILADELPHIA 1815

Approximately two hundred cabinetmakers were working in Baltimore and Annapolis, Maryland, during the Federal Period, according to newspaper listings. Except for John Shaw of Annapolis, most of these skilled workmen are now forgotten. They left a great heritage of furniture distinguished by fine workmanship and superbly executed decoration. Notable among Maryland Federal pieces are sideboards with inlay, and secretaries with glass cupboards. The size of these large pieces was minimized by their excellent proportions. Since Hepplewhite was dominant in Maryland, inlay was used lavishly. Here the bellflower motif was longer-petaled than anywhere else. Eagle and urn were other inlays.

Furniture had flowered in Philadelphia in the years before the Revolution, but about 1800 some notable Sheraton pieces began to appear there. For the rest of the Federal Period, such cabinetmakers as Henry Connelly and Ephraim Haines produced pieces comparing favorably to those of Duncan Phyfe. Tables and chairs with classic lines and motifs are representative of the finest Philadelphia cabinetmakers. A settee with four matching chairs from Philadelphia and a Baltimore secretary were acquired for the recent White House restoration.

SIDE CHAIR of mahogany; urn and drapery carving. Maryland.

SIDE CHAIR, saber legs; carved crest and slat. Philadelphia

SOFA in Sheraton style has inlay typical of Maryland on legs and back frame.

DINING TABLE shows characteristic Hepplewhite details as they were interpreted in Maryland.

SEWING TABLE has octagonal top; reeded legs. Salem, circa 1800.

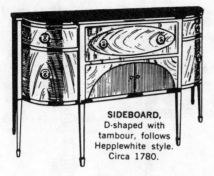

SIDEBOARD, D-shaped with tambour, follows Hepplewhite style. Circa 1780.

CARD TABLE of mahogany was carved by Samuel McIntire. Circa 1800.

SIDE CHAIR by Benjamin Frothingham, carved by Samuel McIntire.

1780 NEW ENGLAND 1815

Massachusetts and particularly the city of Boston had excelled in producing handsome furniture throughout Colonial days. Again during the Federal years, many cabinetmakers and carvers, chairmakers and skilled joiners kept busy not only in Boston but also in small, prosperous towns. In Salem, Nehemiah Adams, Nathaniel Appleton and others turned out furniture to rival that of John Seymour and the Skillin family in Boston. Salem claims Samuel McIntire, who was both a carver and an architect; his inimitable carvings set off furniture made by cabinetmakers in Salem and Boston. Marblehead, Newburyport and Ipswich had stately homes filled with Federal furniture. Benjamin Frothingham of nearby Charlestown turned to the new style, and William Lloyd of Springfield in western Massachusetts is remembered for his inlaid sideboards and graceful card tables. Cabinetmakers in Portsmouth, New Hampshire, often used birch instead of mahogany and those in Connecticut liked cherry, which they inlaid with boxwood or satinwood. New England cabinetmakers followed the classic vogue prevalent everywhere, but gave their splendid bureaus, secretaries, tables, sideboards and serving pieces a distinctly American look.

SECRETARY with roll top, painted glass doors. Salem, circa 1800.

SEWING TABLE has cloth bag under drawers. Salem, circa 1800.

SOFA in Sheraton style has frame carved by Samuel McIntire.

DESK of satinwood with tambour was made by John Seymour of Boston. 1780-1800.

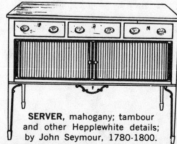

SERVER, mahogany; tambour and other Hepplewhite details; by John Seymour, 1780-1800.

SECRETARY by John Seymour has tambour; urn-shaped keyhole escutcheons; square tapering legs.

ARMCHAIR, "Martha Washington" style in the Sheraton manner. Salem.

SIDEBOARD of mahogany is inlaid and has serpentine front, square tapering legs. Circa 1780.

BUREAU of mahogany and satinwood has matching oval dressing glass. Salem, 1780-1800.

PEG LAMP consists of candlestick and globe to hold oil, with burner; both glass.

LAMP to burn whale oil was made of brass or pewter.

CANDLE SNUFFER, brass, was used to put out flame, trim wick.

MIRROR, urn ornament and side leaves; New England, circa 1785.

MIRROR has painted eagle, cornice frame. New England, circa 1800.

CANDLESTICKS of brass were made in various heights.

MIRROR, surmounted by eagle; gold-leaf frame. New York, circa 1800.

ARGAND LAMP, an improved oil-burning type, gave better light.

DECORATIVE PIECES

City and town houses of the Federal Period were not only furnished more completely than ever before, but the gleaming mahogany and cherry pieces were also supplemented with many smaller things to make living more comfortable. Mirrors were more plentiful and frames displayed details similar to those of Hepplewhite and Sheraton furniture. Many mirrors of the early Federal years had mahogany frames; their ornaments were covered with gold leaf, but after 1800 the entire frame usually was gilded. The two-panel mirror with a reverse painting on the upper piece of glass, which became so popular after 1800, was made in greater quantity than any previous style. New in America about 1800 was the convex looking glass with a circular frame covered with gold leaf; authentic ones have a pendent finial of carved foliage at the base and are usually surmounted by an eagle. Many of these mirrors were the girandole kind, with holders for two or more candles. Tall case or grandfather clocks continued to be made, but after 1800 smaller wall and shelf clocks became more common. Simon Willard of Roxbury, Massachusetts, patented his appealing banjo clock in 1802 and his lighthouse clock a few years later; the latter is now rare. Since candles of better quality were available, fixtures including candlesticks, sconces, lamps, chandeliers and hanging lanterns were made of various materials. The peg lamp and other small lamps to burn whale oil, as well as large improved oil-burning lamps such as the Argand, became quite common. Now, too, more rooms in a house had fireplaces where brass equipment gleamed. Each hearth had andirons and perhaps a fender, tools with brass handles, and brass jamb hooks on which to hang them, all brightly polished.

CLOCK, tall case or grandfather style, by Simon Willard. 1780-1800.

CLOCK, half-high or grandmother type; New England, 1800-1810.

◄ **CLOCK** of mahogany to hang on wall was made by Simon Willard. 1780-1790.

ANDIRONS have brass shafts, urn-shaped finials. Circa 1800.

ANDIRONS with heavier brass shafts were tipped with balls. Circa 1810.

LANTERN to hang indoors was glass, and burned oil.

CLOCK is the lighthouse type, invented by Simon Willard.

The Age of Victoria

EMPIRE *and* VICTORIAN

The massive furniture of the EMPIRE period (1815-1840) and its preferred motifs—the still-popular eagle, flowers, fruits, horns of plenty to signify abundance—reflect a new nation's pride in its growing prosperity. Classic elements persist, but emphasis has shifted from the Greek to the Roman. Wood trim may be carved and gilded to look like metal, or stenciled to give the same effect. At this time power is first applied to woodworking, and Hitchcock chairs, made on a sort of assembly line, become the first mass-produced furniture. Many of the most distinguished cabinetmakers of the Federal era continued to produce during this period, adopting the new style more or less rebelliously, and turning out furniture soundly made of good materials. By the beginning of the VICTORIAN era (1840-1880) America is well-enough established to be able to dream as well as to work, and the prevailing mood is romantic. No true new style appears, but with increasing help from machines all the old ones are interpreted, adapted, combined or borrowed from with a cheerful disregard for accuracy. The result is sometimes absurd but often delightful, and such pieces as John Belter's lacy, gracefully scrolled adaptations of Louis XV are among our most cherished heirlooms.

Secretary. Mahogany; brass mounts and winged-paw feet; marble corner columns.

Wardrobe. Rosewood; carved and gilded; paneled doors.

Console table. Mahogany; marble top and columns; mirror panel at back.

Sofa, Récamier type. Scrolled back, arms, legs; painted black with gilt stenciling. Form and decoration typical of the period.

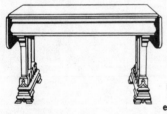

Gothic sofa table. Walnut; drop leaves; supported by columns on bracket feet; ogee-molded drawer in skirt.

Painted iron chair. Velvet upholstery; early contour model.

Gothic side chair. Black walnut; cusped-arch back.

Spool-turned Elizabethan armchair. Walnut; high back.

Reclining chair. Mahogany, velvet; forerunner of Morris chair: adjustable back, footrest.

Acorn mantel or shelf clock. Rosewood; painted glass.

Louis XV medallion-back sofa. Carved serpentine back frame enclosing center medallion, continued to arms.

Louis XV lady rocker. Cherry, horsehair; finger-molded frame.

Armchair, Renaissance with Louis XVI. Mahogany with inlay.

Louis XV gentleman's armchair. Carved rosewood.

Louis XV chair. Walnut, velour; cartouche back.

DICTIONARY OF FURNITURE

Empire

Wall bracket. Carved stars, eagle, foliage.

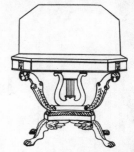

Mirror clock. Floral decoration around dial, corner rosettes; spool-turned frame.

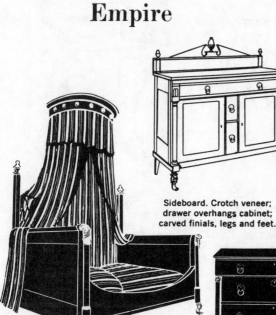

Sideboard. Crotch veneer; drawer overhangs cabinet; carved finials, legs and feet.

Elbow chair. Mahogany; scrolled back and arms, turned legs.

Hitchcock chair. Eagle slat, cut out and stenciled.

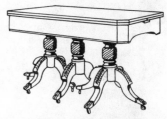

Card table. Canted corners; oversize-lyre support, carved winged-paw feet.

Crown bed. Mahogany; copied from contemporary French model. Empire pieces are well made, of good materials.

Chest of drawers. Overhanging top drawer, corner columns; brass rosette ring pulls.

Pedestal-base center table. Marble top; brass paw feet and casters.

Three-pedestal dining table. Opens to double size; pedestal shafts spiral reeded.

Victorian

Louis XV center table, Belter type. Black walnut, marble; scrolled, carved.

Small stand. Mother-of-pearl inlaid and gilded.

Drop-front desk with whatnot. Louis XV curves with Jacobean spindles.

Renaissance sideboard. Black walnut with marble; high shaped pediment, arched top.

Gothic cupboard-base whatnot. Pierced trim.

Gothic paneled bed. Mahogany; octagonal posts; paneled and arched headboard, foot-board, side pieces; elaborate finials.

Spool bed. Spool-turned posts, spindles, headboard and footboard; squared corner sections; ball-and-ring turned finials.

Louis XV bed, Belter type. Laminated rosewood; carved, pierced, scrolled; quarter-round block feet.

Woman's Day Dictionary of
VICTORIAN FURNITURE

By DOROTHY H. JENKINS

VICTORIAN RENAISSANCE
Wardrobe has two
mirror panels; the fruit and
foliage carving at top
is flanked by carved acroteria.

VICTORIAN ROCOCO
Davenport (or small desk) is
named for man who designed it,
the front legs are carved.

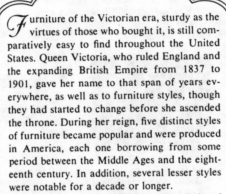

*F*urniture of the Victorian era, sturdy as the virtues of those who bought it, is still comparatively easy to find throughout the United States. Queen Victoria, who ruled England and the expanding British Empire from 1837 to 1901, gave her name to that span of years everywhere, as well as to furniture styles, though they had started to change before she ascended the throne. During her reign, five distinct styles of furniture became popular and were produced in America, each one borrowing from some period between the Middle Ages and the eighteenth century. In addition, several lesser styles were notable for a decade or longer.

In the 1830's cabinetmakers still produced most of the furniture to order, at least in cities. In each succeeding decade, however, more furniture was made in factories. Most Victorian furniture was well built, much of it from fine hardwoods. Carving was universal, at first in high relief but in later years shallow or incised. Mirrors, like marble tops, decorated every possible piece. Victorians loved sets of furniture and bought appropriate ones for parlors, dining rooms and bedrooms. Two new pieces, the whatnot for bric-a-brac and the hallstand, a completely American concept, typify the era. On these eight pages we show the diverse, grand and sometimes gaudily ornate styles of the Victorian years, all reflecting the vigorous individuality and experimentation that were characteristic of nineteenth-century America.

Illustrations by HELEN DISBROW

VICTORIAN TRANSITIONAL
Center table, which once occupied
center-stage in the living room,
has marble top, scrolled pedestal.

VICTORIAN EASTLAKE (JACOBEAN)
Commode, walnut with burl
veneer panels, has marble top,
brass drawer pulls.

VICTORIAN MEDLEY (BENTWOOD)
Rocking chair with laminated birchwood
frame, cane seat and back,
was made after 1859.

VICTORIAN GOTHIC
Bed has headboard and footboard
carved to form graceful arches.

**VICTORIAN
RENAISSANCE**
Sofa is derived from
eighteenth-century
French Louis XVI piece.

MORE ▶

VICTORIAN TRANSITIONAL
1830's - 1840's

Cabinetmakers during the 1830's continued to use mahogany for the imposing furniture of the American Empire period (1815-1840). But while outlines and proportions remained the same, details began to change, thus creating a transition between American Empire and true Victorian. Chairs, for example, usually had saber legs (front ones curved forward, rear ones backward), an American Empire characteristic; but crest rails began to show carving.

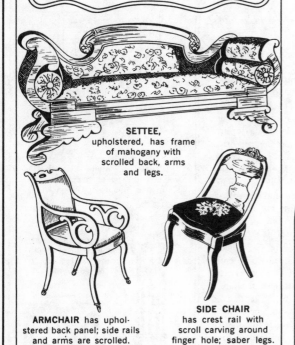

SETTEE, upholstered, has frame of mahogany with scrolled back, arms and legs.

ARMCHAIR has upholstered back panel; side rails and arms are scrolled.

SIDE CHAIR has crest rail with scroll carving around finger hole; saber legs.

HALLSTAND, fancifully carved, has small mirror, pegs for clothing, umbrella racks at sides.

HALLSTAND has quatrefoil and crocket carving, mirror above marble shelf, drip pan for umbrellas.

VICTORIAN GOTHIC
1830's *1850's*

One of the most distinctive styles of the long era, Victorian Gothic, began to emerge by the late 1830's. It was inspired by the Gothic revival in architecture which followed the neoclassic years of the early nineteenth century. In fact, some architects of Gothic-revival buildings designed appropriate furniture for them. Victorian Gothic furniture is easy to recognize, for chair backs as well as headboards and footboards of beds displayed the tracery of Gothic arches. Other typical motifs were quatrefoils, trefoils, rosettes, heraldic devices and crockets. Chair backs were carved and pierced in a variety of designs. Tables and sofas, popular throughout the Victorian age, seem to be the only important pieces that escaped the Gothic revival. With these exceptions, Gothic motifs and tracery were adapted to everything from mirrors to hallstands. The hallstand, also called a hat rack; hatstand, hat tree or hall tree, made its appearance at this time. A high, narrow piece for hats, outer clothing and umbrellas, it usually had a mirror too.

SIDE CHAIR has tall carved back surmounted with finials; square legs.

WHATNOT has cupboard base with Gothic panels, carved supports for shelves.

SIDE CHAIR rosewood, has upholstered back and seat; an open quatrefoil is carved under the finial.

DESK, flat-topped, has front panels carved with heraldic devices.

SIDE CHAIR, rosewood, has back carved in tracery of Gothic arches, flat cabriole front legs.

CABINET is made of rosewood with tulipwood-and-ebony inlay; the panels and other architectural details are typically Renaissance.

SMALL TABLE has inlaid top, pillar-and-cross base, angular braces.

SIDE CHAIR has upholstered seat and back, scroll-carved uprights.

SIDE TABLE, its wood top edged with marquetry, has legs carved as columns, vase final on stretcher.

ARMCHAIR, known as an easy chair because of its deep upholstery, has walnut frame; it matches the side chair above.

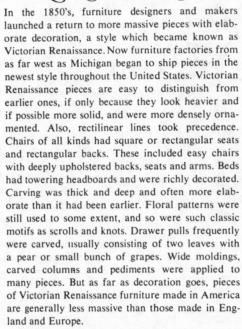

VICTORIAN
1855 RENAISSANCE 1875

In the 1850's, furniture designers and makers launched a return to more massive pieces with elaborate decoration, a style which became known as Victorian Renaissance. Now furniture factories from as far west as Michigan began to ship pieces in the newest style throughout the United States. Victorian Renaissance pieces are easy to distinguish from earlier ones, if only because they look heavier and if possible more solid, and were more densely ornamented. Also, rectilinear lines took precedence. Chairs of all kinds had square or rectangular seats and rectangular backs. These included easy chairs with deeply upholstered backs, seats and arms. Beds had towering headboards and were richly decorated. Carving was thick and deep and often more elaborate than it had been earlier. Floral patterns were still used to some extent, and so were such classic motifs as scrolls and knots. Drawer pulls frequently were carved, usually consisting of two leaves with a pear or small bunch of grapes. Wide moldings, carved columns and pediments were applied to many pieces. But as far as decoration goes, pieces of Victorian Renaissance furniture made in America are generally less massive than those made in England and Europe.

Common pieces were an imposing sideboard with marble top and high backboard that supported small shelves, as well as dining tables and parlor tables, usually oblong or round with a pedestal base. Marble tops somehow seemed to suit these weighty Victorian Renaissance pieces, and of the many colors available, the white, white-and-gray and pink-and-chocolate marbles were the favorites everywhere.

SIDE CHAIR has upholstered seat, high back with carved interlaced splat.

COMMODE, made of black walnut with applied panels of burl walnut, has mushroom-turned knobs.

STAND for vase or lamp is small and higher than average; the painted top is removable.

SMALL STAND has top and shelves of marble; the low glass shelf is framed in metal.

SIDEBOARD with marble top, paneled cupboard and back has a pediment and small shelf.

BED has headboard towering over footboard; both are paneled and display applied moldings.

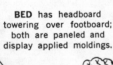

SETTEE, part of a parlor set, has upholstered back, arms and seat; the walnut frame is carved.

CURULE ARMCHAIR, walnut, has semicircular segments instead of legs, upholstered seat, back and armrests.

VICTORIAN ROCOCO

1840's — *1860's*

A lighter and more graceful style, Victorian Rococo was the most important of the many styles in this era and perhaps the most attractive. Also known as Victorian Louis XV, Rococo pieces displayed the curving lines and scrolls, cabriole legs and carving that distinguished eighteenth-century Louis XV furniture. For Victorian Louis XV pieces, roses and other flowers, grapes, leaves and sometimes birds were the choices for carving. Often combined with the carving was deep finger molding. Backs of chairs in a parlor set were oval as was the white marble top on the center table. Also oval were the backs of that peculiarly Victorian pair of chairs, the husband-and-wife or lady-and-gentleman chairs. The man's was larger and had arms; the lady's was armless and hence comfortable to sit in while sewing. The étagère, a variation of the simple whatnot, consisted of a large mirror flanked by small graduated shelves.

John Belter of New York City shipped his Rococo tables, chairs and sofas all over the country; his process for laminating wood permitted it to be shaped and also carved in intricate designs. Among other distinguished cabinetmakers were Elijah Galusha of Troy, New York; François Seignouret and Prudent Mallard of New Orleans.

COMMODE from bedroom set by Prudent Mallard has marble top, shelves across back.

TÊTE-À-TÊTE SOFA, laminated rosewood, permits two persons to sit facing each other.

BED by John Belter is laminated rosewood curved and carved with flowers and foliage.

BED by Prudent Mallard has shaped headboard and footboard; half-tester on posts is added to headboard.

DRESSING TABLE by Prudent Mallard has small marble-topped drawers flanking the mirror.

CENTER TABLE by François Seignouret has rosewood top, leaf-carved legs, hoof feet.

CONSOLE TABLE, part of a parlor set, has marble top, cabriole legs with shell-carved knees.

HUSBAND-WIFE CHAIRS, the man's slightly larger and higher than the lady's, have balloon backs (oval frames).

SIDE CHAIR, black walnut, has bunch of grapes carved on crest rail.

SIDE CHAIR by John Belter is laminated rosewood with grape and scroll carving.

CENTER TABLE by John Belter, laminated rosewood, has detailed carving.

SOFA, rosewood frame, has scroll and foliage carving; upholstered arms curve into back.

ARMCHAIR by John Belter is laminated rosewood with naturalistic carving.

VICTORIAN ROCOCO *continued*

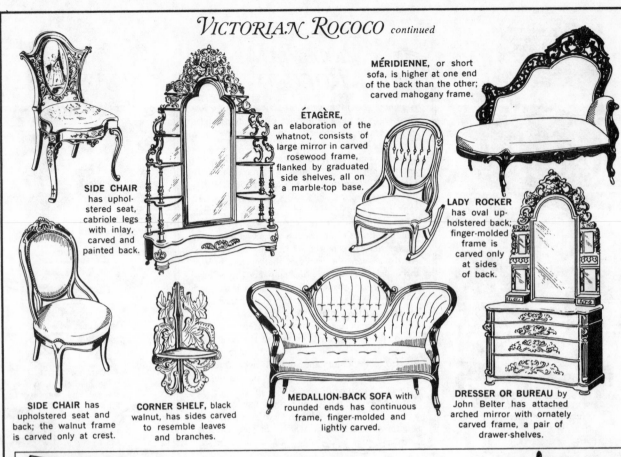

SIDE CHAIR has upholstered seat, cabriole legs with inlay, carved and painted back.

ÉTAGÈRE, an elaboration of the whatnot, consists of large mirror in carved rosewood frame, flanked by graduated side shelves, all on a marble-top base.

MÉRIDIENNE, or short sofa, is higher at one end of the back than the other; carved mahogany frame.

LADY ROCKER has oval upholstered back; finger-molded frame is carved only at sides of back.

SIDE CHAIR has upholstered seat and back; the walnut frame is carved only at crest.

CORNER SHELF, black walnut, has sides carved to resemble leaves and branches.

MEDALLION-BACK SOFA with rounded ends has continuous frame, finger-molded and lightly carved.

DRESSER OR BUREAU by John Belter has attached arched mirror with ornately carved frame, a pair of drawer-shelves.

VICTORIAN *Eastlake*

1870   1900

A plea for simplicity in the book *Hints on Household Taste* by Charles Locke Eastlake, first published in the United States in 1872, inspired American furniture manufacturers to produce enormous amounts of black walnut and oak pieces of fairly plain, angular construction, decorated rather simply with incising. This was known as Victorian Eastlake or, sometimes, Victorian Jacobean. Sprigs of flowers were cut in outline instead of relief. Sets for parlors, dining rooms and bedrooms often had aprons and shelves with gingerbread edges. Emphasis was often on quantity, not quality.

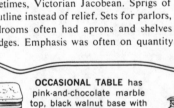

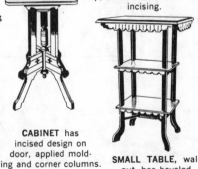

SECRETARY is black walnut; its roll top has been removed to provide storage space.

OCCASIONAL TABLE has pink-and-chocolate marble top, black walnut base with incising.

SIDEBOARD has paneled cupboards below, shelves above and cupboard for tableware.

CABINET has incised design on door, applied molding and corner columns.

SMALL TABLE, walnut, has beveled edges and gingerbread aprons.

CYLINDER-TOP DESK, black walnut, has incised decoration, veneer panels, beveled edges.

ARMCHAIR with upholstered seat and back panel has black walnut frame.

SIDE CHAIR by Hitchcock is painted black and stenciled, has cane seat.

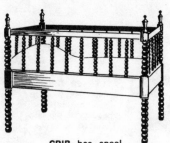

CRIB has spool-turned legs and spindles around sides, vase-turned finials.

CRADLE ROCKER in the Hitchcock style has seating space for one adult; baby sleeps behind rail.

BEDSIDE TABLE, maple, has spool-turned legs, one drawer with glass knob.

WHATNOT, black walnut, has spool-turned uprights between graduated shelves.

SMALL TABLE is trestle type with spool-turned uprights and scrolled feet.

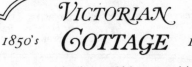

VICTORIAN COTTAGE

1850's — 1880's

Cottage or country furniture, which appeared in many different styles during the Victorian years, was of plain construction and was often made of a cheap softwood, then painted or enameled in various colors. Simple painted furniture which could be easily mass-produced and was therefore inexpensive had been advocated by Andrew J. Downing in his book *Architecture of Country Houses,* published in 1850.

Previous to 1850, Lambert Hitchcock's name had become synonymous with any light painted chair with stenciled decoration made between 1825 and 1860. The style of chair that bears his name first came from his factory in Hitchcocksville, Connecticut, where it was made by hand but was cut, turned, assembled, painted and stenciled in assembly-line fashion. The chairs were shipped to other parts of the country, and soon other furniture makers were copying the Hitchcock chair. This style is recognized by its rectangular back which usually has one or more horizontal splats and a wide crest rail, legs and stretchers with simple turnings, and a square rush or cane seat. All wood parts were painted redbrown or black, and gold stencil decoration was applied to the splat and crest rail.

The most popular style of Cottage furniture was the spool-turned variety produced chiefly between 1850 and 1865 and in smaller quantity until about 1880. The name Jenny Lind became associated with this type of furniture because it first gained popularity when the famous singer was touring the United States. The term "spool" or "bobbin" is most descriptive of the turning done on the straight members of each piece, such as spindles, railings and bars, although some turnings resemble knobs or buttons. This type of turning represents a revival in the United States of Elizabethan spiral twisting in simplified form. Whatnots, beds, small tables for various uses, small chairs, washstands and towel racks for bedrooms were important and common spool-turned pieces.

ARMCHAIR, walnut with cushioned seat, back and armrests, has spool-turned legs, uprights and spindles.

WASHSTAND has spool-turned legs and towel bars on sides, one drawer.

BED has spool-turned spindles and rails in headboard and footboard.

CENTER TABLE has round white marble top, black walnut pedestal.

WHATNOT is black walnut with carved crest, turned uprights between shelves.

COMMODE is maple with white marble top; drawer pulls are carved in the shape of leaves.

CENTER TABLE, Thonet bentwood, has solid oval top; the pedestal is typically shaped bentwood.

SIDE CHAIR, upholstered, is made of cast and wrought iron; the crown-shaped wrought-iron base acts as a spring, allowing the sitter to move or recline.

SIDE CHAIR reflects the plain construction preferred by Eastlake; it has an ebonized frame, flower inlay.

DRESSING STAND, Thonet, has bentwood frame and support for mirror on bentwood table.

HALLSTAND has Rococo scrolls ending in pegs, a drip pan below for umbrellas; cast iron forms the standard and frames the small mirror.

1840 VICTORIAN

Victorian homes were as crammed with furniture as their whatnots and mantelpieces were with bric-a-brac, and the taste in both furniture and bric-a-brac was catholic. By the 1880's it was not unusual for a family sitting room to be decorated in the Turkish manner—as interpreted by American furniture manufacturers—while the rest of the house was furnished with anything from Rococo to Eastlake-inspired pieces.

The desire for novelty and a fascination with mechanical devices led to new innovative furniture. Chairs now reclined, swiveled or folded up. Couches and cupboards miraculously converted into beds. Intricate furniture machinery now made it possible to experiment with new materials. Cane (wicker or rattan) was imported and fashioned into chairs and settees. Bamboo or bamboo-turned wood pieces became popular, particularly in the 1870's when the Orient became a source of interest and inspiration. Furniture reflecting Turkish influence, popular between 1870 and 1880, may be traced to the opening of the Suez Canal and to interest in Mohammedan architecture and art. Sofas, couches and ottomans, and sets consisting of side chairs and armchairs were made for parlor, sitting room and library. Frames were smothered with upholstery which was enhanced with tufting, buttons and fringes.

Cast-iron settees, chairs and tables for gardens were being mass-produced from molds by 1840. Naturalistic patterns emphasizing grapes, lilies of the valley, vines or ferns

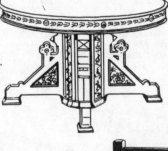

DINING TABLE, oak, is round, has extension leaves; Eastlake influence shows in angular treatment of pillar support and in flattened legs.

ARMCHAIR, Turkish style, has ebonized wood frame; the upholstered seat and headrest are edged with thick fringe.

SECRETARY BOOKCASE, golden oak, has restrained carving; the bookcase is protected by a full-length glass door.

TILT-TOP TABLE is papier-mâché; the top displays a painting framed with gilt and mother-of-pearl inlay.

SIDE CHAIR in original Mission style has a substantial oak frame and square rush seat; this style was later adapted to many pieces, large and small.

ROCKING CHAIR can be folded, has maple frame, beech rockers, upholstered seat and back; it was factory-made for city and country homes.

SETTEE with wicker woven to form frame is a turn-of-the century style, has upholstered seat with cushion.

MORRIS CHAIR with golden oak frame has an adjustable back, tufted cushions for seat and back.

MEDLEY 1900

were most popular, although some designs were based on scrolls. Scroll designs were preferred for the indoor pieces, such as hat racks, mirror frames, small tables, plant stands and beds, that began to appear in the 1850's. Of the indoor pieces, the iron bed remained popular longest, culminating in the brass bedstead of the 1890's.

Papier-mâché pieces also were important throughout the Victorian era. A few pieces were produced in the United States, but most of them were imported from England and France. Papier-mâché was a surprisingly durable material in spite of being made from paper and glue. Many small tables and chairs, which were the most important pieces of this type, were lacquered and also decorated with gilt and mother-of-pearl.

The bentwood process, developed by Michael Thonet in Austria in the 1850's, made possible a side chair that has gained worldwide renown. It has outcurving legs, curved back members, a solid round seat. Bentwood, which was birchwood laminated and bent by steaming, gave fanciful lines and shapes to other pieces of furniture including rocking chairs, tables and dressing stands. This furniture was imported.

One of the last innovations was Mission furniture, which originated in San Francisco. The first pieces were oak chairs of simple design that managed to reflect California's Spanish heritage; these were made by members of the congregation for their church. When they were manufactured commercially of fumed oak, quality declined.

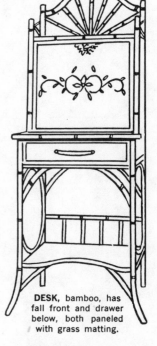

DESK, bamboo, has fall front and drawer below, both paneled with grass matting.

SIDE CHAIR has caned seat; papier-mâché frame is lacquered black and inlaid with mother-of-pearl.

TABOURET, Moorish, has hexagonal top and sides, light wood inlay; sections of the base are cut out in Moorish arches.

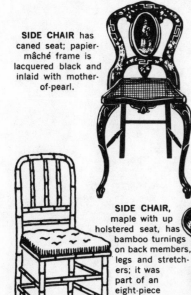

SIDE CHAIR, maple with upholstered seat, has bamboo turnings on back members, legs and stretchers; it was part of an eight-piece bedroom set.

SETTEE, cast iron with slatted seat, was made for garden use; back and trestle supports are in fern pattern.

CIRCULAR SOFA, also called an ottoman (in honor of its Turkish antecedents) or a sociable, has a flat center pedestal used for a potted plant; it has an upholstered seat, back cushions, a carved wood base. Also made in octagonal shape.

Country and
Painted Furniture

EARLY AMERICAN AND
COUNTRY FURNITURE

WINDSORS

COUNTRY STYLES

DICTIONARY OF
EARLY AMERICAN & COUNTRY FURNITURE

By DOROTHY H. JENKINS

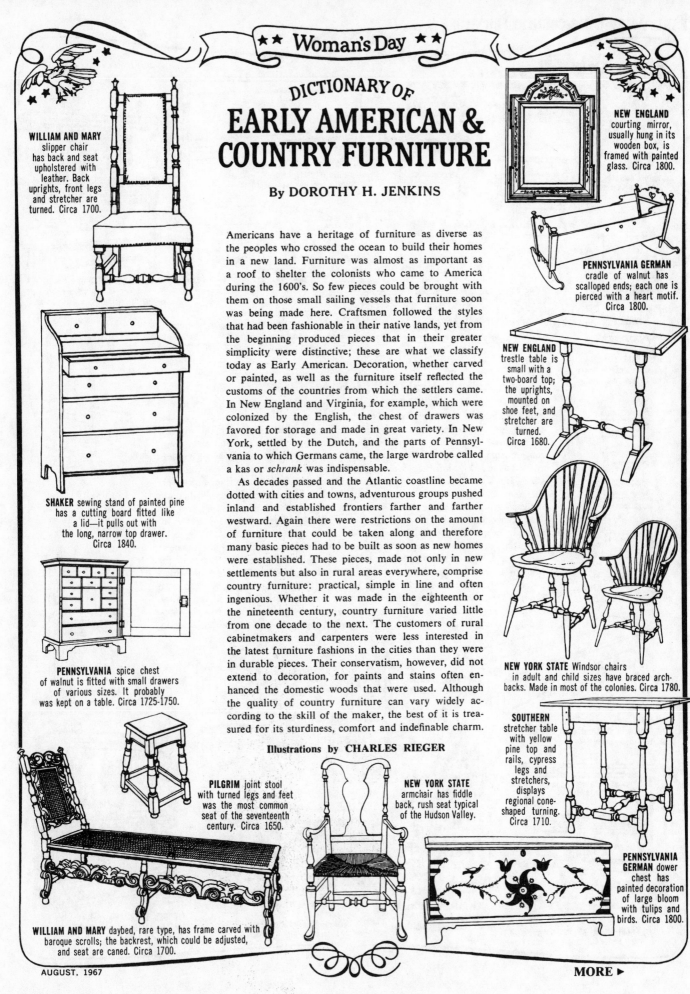

Americans have a heritage of furniture as diverse as the peoples who crossed the ocean to build their homes in a new land. Furniture was almost as important as a roof to shelter the colonists who came to America during the 1600's. So few pieces could be brought with them on those small sailing vessels that furniture soon was being made here. Craftsmen followed the styles that had been fashionable in their native lands, yet from the beginning produced pieces that in their greater simplicity were distinctive; these are what we classify today as Early American. Decoration, whether carved or painted, as well as the furniture itself reflected the customs of the countries from which the settlers came. In New England and Virginia, for example, which were colonized by the English, the chest of drawers was favored for storage and made in great variety. In New York, settled by the Dutch, and the parts of Pennsylvania to which Germans came, the large wardrobe called a kas or *schrank* was indispensable.

As decades passed and the Atlantic coastline became dotted with cities and towns, adventurous groups pushed inland and established frontiers farther and farther westward. Again there were restrictions on the amount of furniture that could be taken along and therefore many basic pieces had to be built as soon as new homes were established. These pieces, made not only in new settlements but also in rural areas everywhere, comprise country furniture: practical, simple in line and often ingenious. Whether it was made in the eighteenth or the nineteenth century, country furniture varied little from one decade to the next. The customers of rural cabinetmakers and carpenters were less interested in the latest furniture fashions in the cities than they were in durable pieces. Their conservatism, however, did not extend to decoration, for paints and stains often enhanced the domestic woods that were used. Although the quality of country furniture can vary widely according to the skill of the maker, the best of it is treasured for its sturdiness, comfort and indefinable charm.

Illustrations by CHARLES RIEGER

WILLIAM AND MARY slipper chair has back and seat upholstered with leather. Back uprights, front legs and stretcher are turned. Circa 1700.

SHAKER sewing stand of painted pine has a cutting board fitted like a lid—it pulls out with the long, narrow top drawer. Circa 1840.

PENNSYLVANIA spice chest of walnut is fitted with small drawers of various sizes. It probably was kept on a table. Circa 1725-1750.

PILGRIM joint stool with turned legs and feet was the most common seat of the seventeenth century. Circa 1650.

WILLIAM AND MARY daybed, rare type, has frame carved with baroque scrolls; the backrest, which could be adjusted, and seat are caned. Circa 1700.

NEW YORK STATE armchair has fiddle back, rush seat typical of the Hudson Valley.

NEW ENGLAND courting mirror, usually hung in its wooden box, is framed with painted glass. Circa 1800.

PENNSYLVANIA GERMAN cradle of walnut has scalloped ends; each one is pierced with a heart motif. Circa 1800.

NEW ENGLAND trestle table is small with a two-board top; the uprights, mounted on shoe feet, and stretcher are turned. Circa 1680.

NEW YORK STATE Windsor chairs in adult and child sizes have braced arch-backs. Made in most of the colonies. Circa 1780.

SOUTHERN stretcher table with yellow pine top and rails, cypress legs and stretchers, displays regional cone-shaped turning. Circa 1710.

PENNSYLVANIA GERMAN dower chest has painted decoration of large bloom with tulips and birds. Circa 1800.

MORE ▶

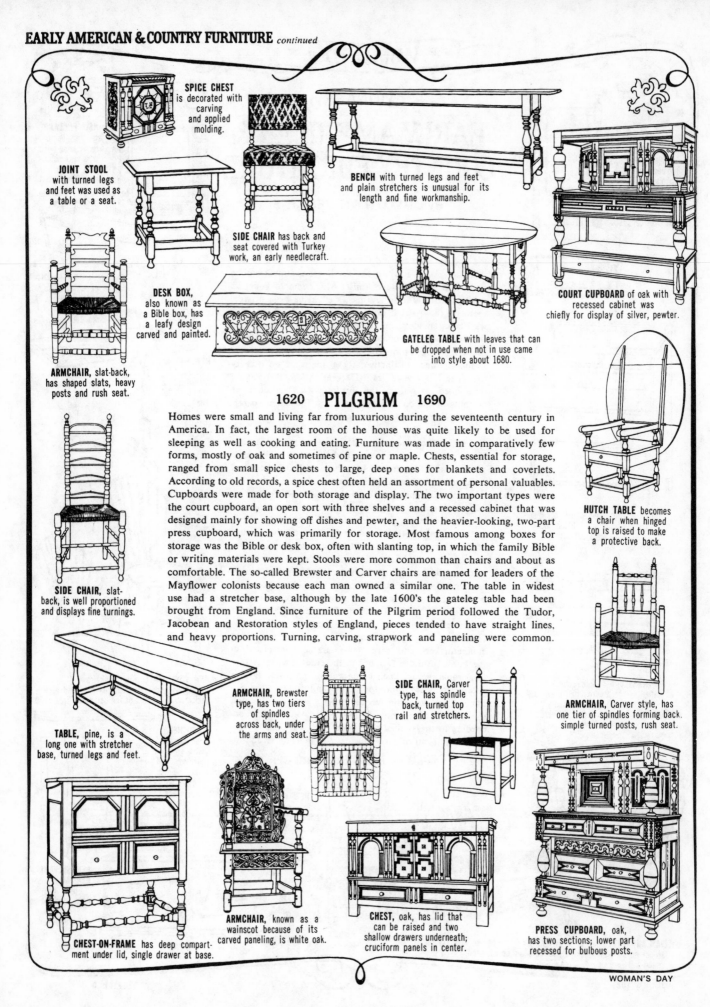

SPICE CHEST is decorated with carving and applied molding.

JOINT STOOL with turned legs and feet was used as a table or a seat.

BENCH with turned legs and feet and plain stretchers is unusual for its length and fine workmanship.

SIDE CHAIR has back and seat covered with Turkey work, an early needlecraft.

DESK BOX, also known as a Bible box, has a leafy design carved and painted.

ARMCHAIR, slat-back, has shaped slats, heavy posts and rush seat.

GATELEG TABLE with leaves that can be dropped when not in use came into style about 1680.

COURT CUPBOARD of oak with recessed cabinet was chiefly for display of silver, pewter.

SIDE CHAIR, slat-back, is well proportioned and displays fine turnings.

1620 PILGRIM 1690

Homes were small and living far from luxurious during the seventeenth century in America. In fact, the largest room of the house was quite likely to be used for sleeping as well as cooking and eating. Furniture was made in comparatively few forms, mostly of oak and sometimes of pine or maple. Chests, essential for storage, ranged from small spice chests to large, deep ones for blankets and coverlets. According to old records, a spice chest often held an assortment of personal valuables. Cupboards were made for both storage and display. The two important types were the court cupboard, an open sort with three shelves and a recessed cabinet that was designed mainly for showing off dishes and pewter, and the heavier-looking, two-part press cupboard, which was primarily for storage. Most famous among boxes for storage was the Bible or desk box, often with slanting top, in which the family Bible or writing materials were kept. Stools were more common than chairs and about as comfortable. The so-called Brewster and Carver chairs are named for leaders of the Mayflower colonists because each man owned a similar one. The table in widest use had a stretcher base, although by the late 1600's the gateleg table had been brought from England. Since furniture of the Pilgrim period followed the Tudor, Jacobean and Restoration styles of England, pieces tended to have straight lines, and heavy proportions. Turning, carving, strapwork and paneling were common.

HUTCH TABLE becomes a chair when hinged top is raised to make a protective back.

TABLE, pine, is a long one with stretcher base, turned legs and feet.

ARMCHAIR, Brewster type, has two tiers of spindles across back, under the arms and seat.

SIDE CHAIR, Carver type, has spindle back, turned top rail and stretchers.

ARMCHAIR, Carver style, has one tier of spindles forming back, simple turned posts, rush seat.

CHEST-ON-FRAME has deep compartment under lid, single drawer at base.

ARMCHAIR, known as a wainscot because of its carved paneling, is white oak.

CHEST, oak, has lid that can be raised and two shallow drawers underneath; cruciform panels in center.

PRESS CUPBOARD, oak, has two sections; lower part recessed for bulbous posts.

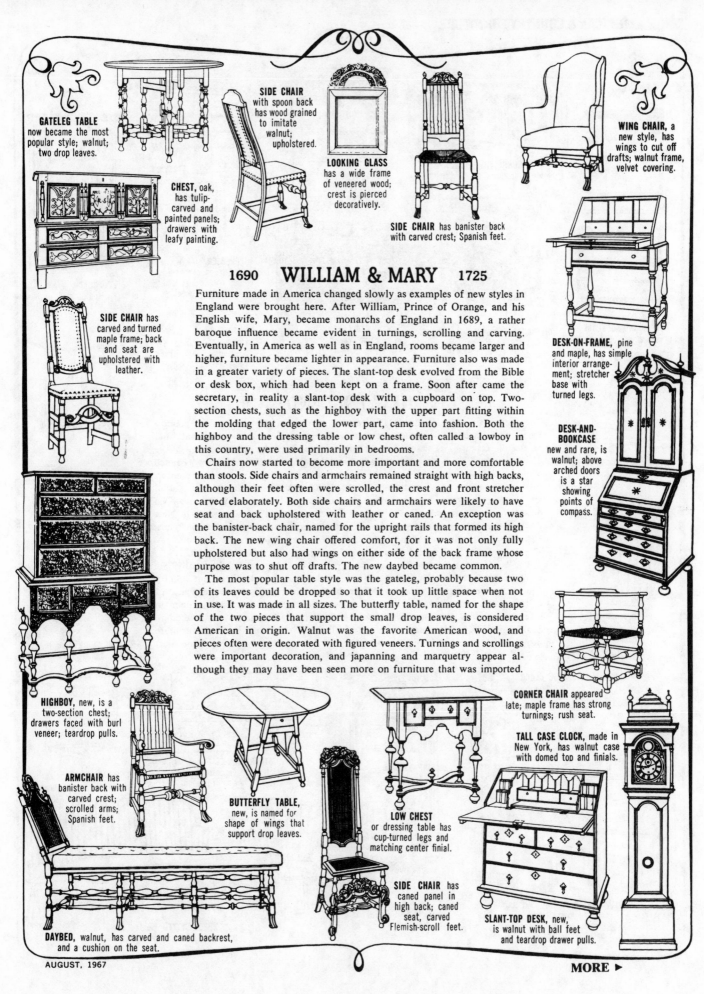

GATELEG TABLE now became the most popular style; walnut; two drop leaves.

SIDE CHAIR with spoon back has wood grained to imitate walnut; upholstered.

LOOKING GLASS has a wide frame of veneered wood; crest is pierced decoratively.

WING CHAIR, a new style, has wings to cut off drafts; walnut frame, velvet covering.

CHEST, oak, has tulip-carved and painted panels; drawers with leafy painting.

SIDE CHAIR has banister back with carved crest; Spanish feet.

SIDE CHAIR has carved and turned maple frame; back and seat are upholstered with leather.

1690 WILLIAM & MARY 1725

Furniture made in America changed slowly as examples of new styles in England were brought here. After William, Prince of Orange, and his English wife, Mary, became monarchs of England in 1689, a rather baroque influence became evident in turnings, scrolling and carving. Eventually, in America as well as in England, rooms became larger and higher, furniture became lighter in appearance. Furniture also was made in a greater variety of pieces. The slant-top desk evolved from the Bible or desk box, which had been kept on a frame. Soon after came the secretary, in reality a slant-top desk with a cupboard on top. Two-section chests, such as the highboy with the upper part fitting within the molding that edged the lower part, came into fashion. Both the highboy and the dressing table or low chest, often called a lowboy in this country, were used primarily in bedrooms.

Chairs now started to become more important and more comfortable than stools. Side chairs and armchairs remained straight with high backs, although their feet often were scrolled, the crest and front stretcher carved elaborately. Both side chairs and armchairs were likely to have seat and back upholstered with leather or caned. An exception was the banister-back chair, named for the upright rails that formed its high back. The new wing chair offered comfort, for it was not only fully upholstered but also had wings on either side of the back frame whose purpose was to shut off drafts. The new daybed became common.

The most popular table style was the gateleg, probably because two of its leaves could be dropped so that it took up little space when not in use. It was made in all sizes. The butterfly table, named for the shape of the two pieces that support the small drop leaves, is considered American in origin. Walnut was the favorite American wood, and pieces often were decorated with figured veneers. Turnings and scrollings were important decoration, and japanning and marquetry appear although they may have been seen more on furniture that was imported.

DESK-ON-FRAME, pine and maple, has simple interior arrangement; stretcher base with turned legs.

DESK-AND-BOOKCASE new and rare, is walnut; above arched doors is a star showing points of compass.

HIGHBOY, new, is a two-section chest; drawers faced with burl veneer; teardrop pulls.

ARMCHAIR has banister back with carved crest; scrolled arms; Spanish feet.

BUTTERFLY TABLE, new, is named for shape of wings that support drop leaves.

CORNER CHAIR appeared late; maple frame has strong turnings; rush seat.

TALL CASE CLOCK, made in New York, has walnut case with domed top and finials.

LOW CHEST or dressing table has cup-turned legs and matching center finial.

SIDE CHAIR has caned panel in high back; caned seat, carved Flemish-scroll feet.

SLANT-TOP DESK, new, is walnut with ball feet and teardrop drawer pulls.

DAYBED, walnut, has carved and caned backrest, and a cushion on the seat.

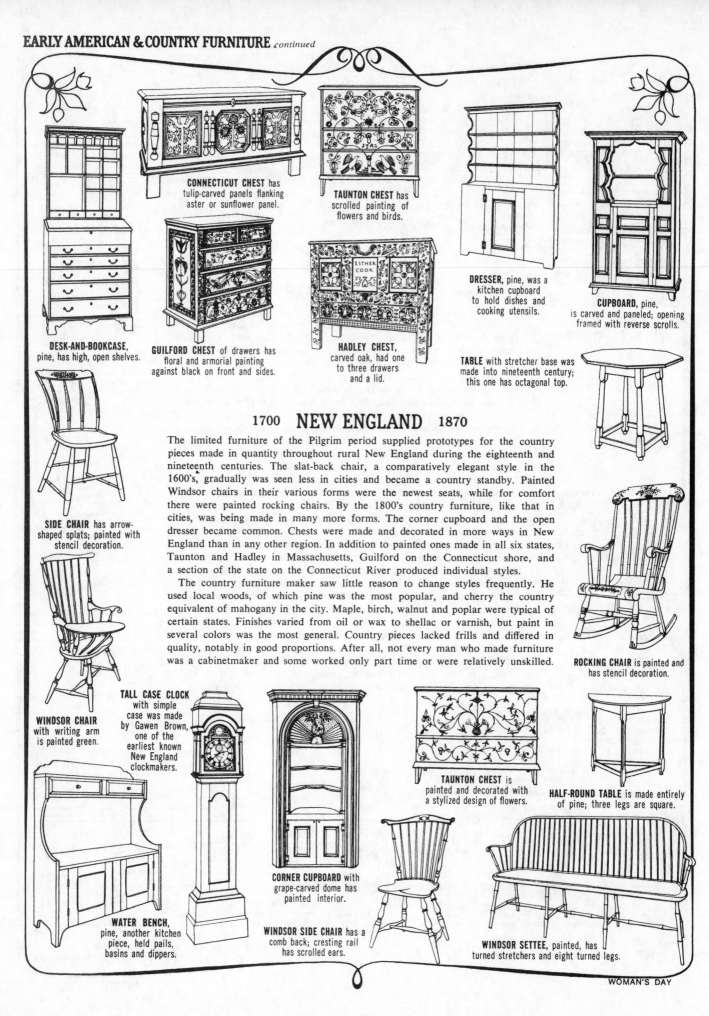

CONNECTICUT CHEST has tulip-carved panels flanking aster or sunflower panel.

TAUNTON CHEST has scrolled painting of flowers and birds.

DRESSER, pine, was a kitchen cupboard to hold dishes and cooking utensils.

CUPBOARD, pine, is carved and paneled; opening framed with reverse scrolls.

DESK-AND-BOOKCASE, pine, has high, open shelves.

GUILFORD CHEST of drawers has floral and armorial painting against black on front and sides.

HADLEY CHEST, carved oak, had one to three drawers and a lid.

TABLE with stretcher base was made into nineteenth century; this one has octagonal top.

SIDE CHAIR has arrow-shaped splats; painted with stencil decoration.

1700 NEW ENGLAND 1870

The limited furniture of the Pilgrim period supplied prototypes for the country pieces made in quantity throughout rural New England during the eighteenth and nineteenth centuries. The slat-back chair, a comparatively elegant style in the 1600's, gradually was seen less in cities and became a country standby. Painted Windsor chairs in their various forms were the newest seats, while for comfort there were painted rocking chairs. By the 1800's country furniture, like that in cities, was being made in many more forms. The corner cupboard and the open dresser became common. Chests were made and decorated in more ways in New England than in any other region. In addition to painted ones made in all six states, Taunton and Hadley in Massachusetts, Guilford on the Connecticut shore, and a section of the state on the Connecticut River produced individual styles.

The country furniture maker saw little reason to change styles frequently. He used local woods, of which pine was the most popular, and cherry the country equivalent of mahogany in the city. Maple, birch, walnut and poplar were typical of certain states. Finishes varied from oil or wax to shellac or varnish, but paint in several colors was the most general. Country pieces lacked frills and differed in quality, notably in good proportions. After all, not every man who made furniture was a cabinetmaker and some worked only part time or were relatively unskilled.

ROCKING CHAIR is painted and has stencil decoration.

WINDSOR CHAIR with writing arm is painted green.

TALL CASE CLOCK with simple case was made by Gawen Brown, one of the earliest known New England clockmakers.

TAUNTON CHEST is painted and decorated with a stylized design of flowers.

HALF-ROUND TABLE is made entirely of pine; three legs are square.

WATER BENCH, pine, another kitchen piece, held pails, basins and dippers.

CORNER CUPBOARD with grape-carved dome has painted interior.

WINDSOR SIDE CHAIR has a comb back; cresting rail has scrolled ears.

WINDSOR SETTEE, painted, has turned stretchers and eight turned legs.

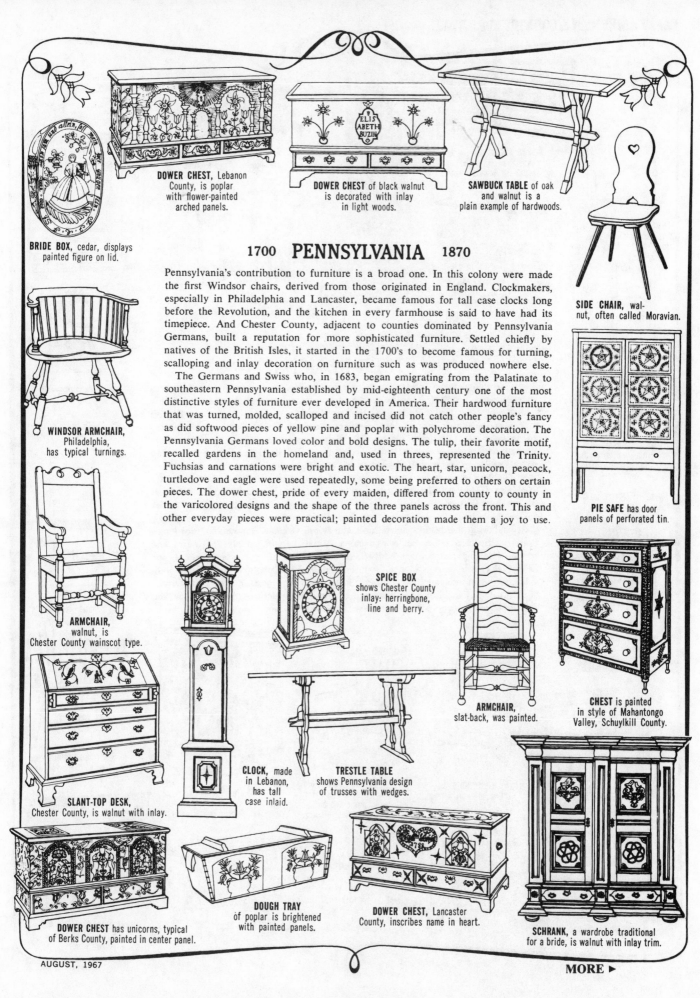

BRIDE BOX, cedar, displays painted figure on lid.

DOWER CHEST, Lebanon County, is poplar with flower-painted arched panels.

DOWER CHEST of black walnut is decorated with inlay in light woods.

SAWBUCK TABLE of oak and walnut is a plain example of hardwoods.

SIDE CHAIR, walnut, often called Moravian.

1700 PENNSYLVANIA 1870

Pennsylvania's contribution to furniture is a broad one. In this colony were made the first Windsor chairs, derived from those originated in England. Clockmakers, especially in Philadelphia and Lancaster, became famous for tall case clocks long before the Revolution, and the kitchen in every farmhouse is said to have had its timepiece. And Chester County, adjacent to counties dominated by Pennsylvania Germans, built a reputation for more sophisticated furniture. Settled chiefly by natives of the British Isles, it started in the 1700's to become famous for turning, scalloping and inlay decoration on furniture such as was produced nowhere else.

The Germans and Swiss who, in 1683, began emigrating from the Palatinate to southeastern Pennsylvania established by mid-eighteenth century one of the most distinctive styles of furniture ever developed in America. Their hardwood furniture that was turned, molded, scalloped and incised did not catch other people's fancy as did softwood pieces of yellow pine and poplar with polychrome decoration. The Pennsylvania Germans loved color and bold designs. The tulip, their favorite motif, recalled gardens in the homeland and, used in threes, represented the Trinity. Fuchsias and carnations were bright and exotic. The heart, star, unicorn, peacock, turtledove and eagle were used repeatedly, some being preferred to others on certain pieces. The dower chest, pride of every maiden, differed from county to county in the varicolored designs and the shape of the three panels across the front. This and other everyday pieces were practical; painted decoration made them a joy to use.

WINDSOR ARMCHAIR, Philadelphia, has typical turnings.

PIE SAFE has door panels of perforated tin.

ARMCHAIR, walnut, is Chester County wainscot type.

SPICE BOX shows Chester County inlay: herringbone, line and berry.

ARMCHAIR, slat-back, was painted.

CHEST is painted in style of Mahantongo Valley, Schuylkill County.

SLANT-TOP DESK, Chester County, is walnut with inlay.

CLOCK, made in Lebanon, has tall case inlaid.

TRESTLE TABLE shows Pennsylvania design of trusses with wedges.

DOWER CHEST has unicorns, typical of Berks County, painted in center panel.

DOUGH TRAY of poplar is brightened with painted panels.

DOWER CHEST, Lancaster County, inscribes name in heart.

SCHRANK, a wardrobe traditional for a bride, is walnut with inlay trim.

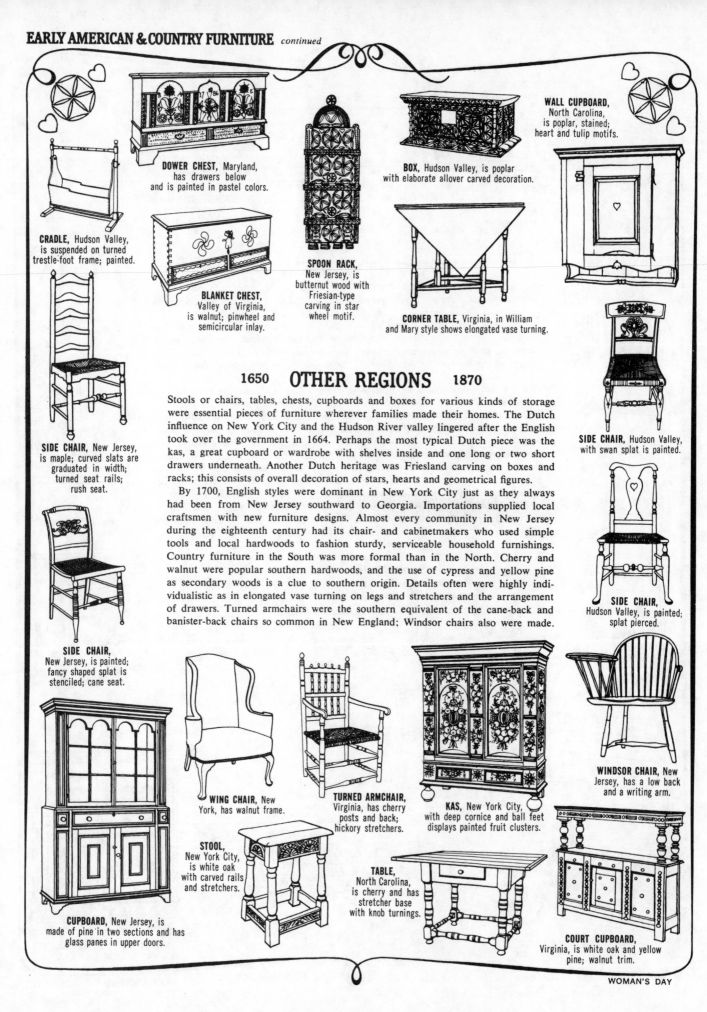

DOWER CHEST, Maryland, has drawers below and is painted in pastel colors.

BOX, Hudson Valley, is poplar with elaborate allover carved decoration.

WALL CUPBOARD, North Carolina, is poplar, stained; heart and tulip motifs.

CRADLE, Hudson Valley, is suspended on turned trestle-foot frame; painted.

BLANKET CHEST, Valley of Virginia, is walnut; pinwheel and semicircular inlay.

SPOON RACK, New Jersey, is butternut wood with Friesian-type carving in star wheel motif.

CORNER TABLE, Virginia, in William and Mary style shows elongated vase turning.

SIDE CHAIR, New Jersey, is maple; curved slats are graduated in width; turned seat rails; rush seat.

SIDE CHAIR, Hudson Valley, with swan splat is painted.

1650 OTHER REGIONS 1870

Stools or chairs, tables, chests, cupboards and boxes for various kinds of storage were essential pieces of furniture wherever families made their homes. The Dutch influence on New York City and the Hudson River valley lingered after the English took over the government in 1664. Perhaps the most typical Dutch piece was the kas, a great cupboard or wardrobe with shelves inside and one long or two short drawers underneath. Another Dutch heritage was Friesland carving on boxes and racks; this consists of overall decoration of stars, hearts and geometrical figures.

By 1700, English styles were dominant in New York City just as they always had been from New Jersey southward to Georgia. Importations supplied local craftsmen with new furniture designs. Almost every community in New Jersey during the eighteenth century had its chair- and cabinetmakers who used simple tools and local hardwoods to fashion sturdy, serviceable household furnishings. Country furniture in the South was more formal than in the North. Cherry and walnut were popular southern hardwoods, and the use of cypress and yellow pine as secondary woods is a clue to southern origin. Details often were highly individualistic as in elongated vase turning on legs and stretchers and the arrangement of drawers. Turned armchairs were the southern equivalent of the cane-back and banister-back chairs so common in New England; Windsor chairs also were made.

SIDE CHAIR, Hudson Valley, is painted; splat pierced.

SIDE CHAIR, New Jersey, is painted; fancy shaped splat is stenciled; cane seat.

WING CHAIR, New York, has walnut frame.

TURNED ARMCHAIR, Virginia, has cherry posts and back; hickory stretchers.

KAS, New York City, with deep cornice and ball feet displays painted fruit clusters.

WINDSOR CHAIR, New Jersey, has a low back and a writing arm.

CUPBOARD, New Jersey, is made of pine in two sections and has glass panes in upper doors.

STOOL, New York City, is white oak with carved rails and stretchers.

TABLE, North Carolina, is cherry and has stretcher base with knob turnings.

COURT CUPBOARD, Virginia, is white oak and yellow pine; walnut trim.

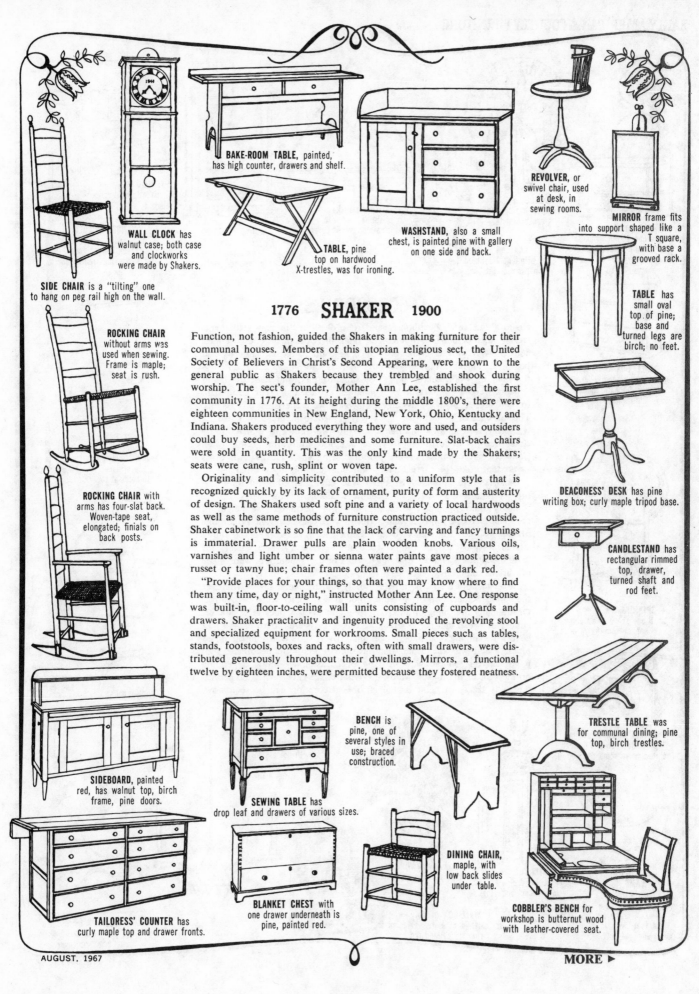

WALL CLOCK has walnut case; both case and clockworks were made by Shakers.

SIDE CHAIR is a "tilting" one to hang on peg rail high on the wall.

ROCKING CHAIR without arms was used when sewing. Frame is maple; seat is rush.

ROCKING CHAIR with arms has four-slat back. Woven-tape seat, elongated; finials on back posts.

BAKE-ROOM TABLE, painted, has high counter, drawers and shelf.

TABLE, pine top on hardwood X-trestles, was for ironing.

WASHSTAND, also a small chest, is painted pine with gallery on one side and back.

REVOLVER, or swivel chair, used at desk, in sewing rooms.

MIRROR frame fits into support shaped like a T square, with base a grooved rack.

TABLE has small oval top of pine; base and turned legs are birch; no feet.

DEACONESS' DESK has pine writing box; curly maple tripod base.

CANDLESTAND has rectangular rimmed top, drawer, turned shaft and rod feet.

1776 SHAKER 1900

Function, not fashion, guided the Shakers in making furniture for their communal houses. Members of this utopian religious sect, the United Society of Believers in Christ's Second Appearing, were known to the general public as Shakers because they trembled and shook during worship. The sect's founder, Mother Ann Lee, established the first community in 1776. At its height during the middle 1800's, there were eighteen communities in New England, New York, Ohio, Kentucky and Indiana. Shakers produced everything they wore and used, and outsiders could buy seeds, herb medicines and some furniture. Slat-back chairs were sold in quantity. This was the only kind made by the Shakers; seats were cane, rush, splint or woven tape.

Originality and simplicity contributed to a uniform style that is recognized quickly by its lack of ornament, purity of form and austerity of design. The Shakers used soft pine and a variety of local hardwoods as well as the same methods of furniture construction practiced outside. Shaker cabinetwork is so fine that the lack of carving and fancy turnings is immaterial. Drawer pulls are plain wooden knobs. Various oils, varnishes and light umber or sienna water paints gave most pieces a russet or tawny hue; chair frames often were painted a dark red.

"Provide places for your things, so that you may know where to find them any time, day or night," instructed Mother Ann Lee. One response was built-in, floor-to-ceiling wall units consisting of cupboards and drawers. Shaker practicality and ingenuity produced the revolving stool and specialized equipment for workrooms. Small pieces such as tables, stands, footstools, boxes and racks, often with small drawers, were distributed generously throughout their dwellings. Mirrors, a functional twelve by eighteen inches, were permitted because they fostered neatness.

SIDEBOARD, painted red, has walnut top, birch frame, pine doors.

SEWING TABLE has drop leaf and drawers of various sizes.

BENCH is pine, one of several styles in use; braced construction.

TRESTLE TABLE was for communal dining; pine top, birch trestles.

TAILORESS' COUNTER has curly maple top and drawer fronts.

BLANKET CHEST with one drawer underneath is pine, painted red.

DINING CHAIR, maple, with low back slides under table.

COBBLER'S BENCH for workshop is butternut wood with leather-covered seat.

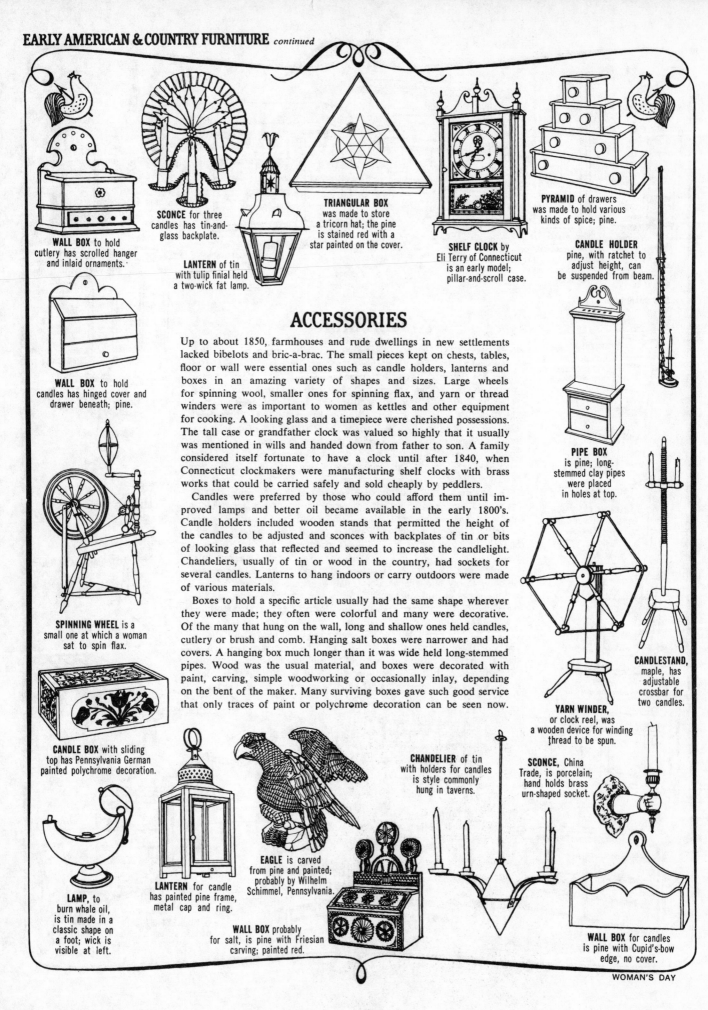

WALL BOX to hold cutlery has scrolled hanger and inlaid ornaments.

SCONCE for three candles has tin-and-glass backplate.

LANTERN of tin with tulip finial held a two-wick fat lamp.

TRIANGULAR BOX was made to store a tricorn hat; the pine is stained red with a star painted on the cover.

SHELF CLOCK by Eli Terry of Connecticut is an early model; pillar-and-scroll case.

PYRAMID of drawers was made to hold various kinds of spice; pine.

CANDLE HOLDER pine, with ratchet to adjust height, can be suspended from beam.

WALL BOX to hold candles has hinged cover and drawer beneath; pine.

ACCESSORIES

Up to about 1850, farmhouses and rude dwellings in new settlements lacked bibelots and bric-a-brac. The small pieces kept on chests, tables, floor or wall were essential ones such as candle holders, lanterns and boxes in an amazing variety of shapes and sizes. Large wheels for spinning wool, smaller ones for spinning flax, and yarn or thread winders were as important to women as kettles and other equipment for cooking. A looking glass and a timepiece were cherished possessions. The tall case or grandfather clock was valued so highly that it usually was mentioned in wills and handed down from father to son. A family considered itself fortunate to have a clock until after 1840, when Connecticut clockmakers were manufacturing shelf clocks with brass works that could be carried safely and sold cheaply by peddlers.

Candles were preferred by those who could afford them until improved lamps and better oil became available in the early 1800's. Candle holders included wooden stands that permitted the height of the candles to be adjusted and sconces with backplates of tin or bits of looking glass that reflected and seemed to increase the candlelight. Chandeliers, usually of tin or wood in the country, had sockets for several candles. Lanterns to hang indoors or carry outdoors were made of various materials.

Boxes to hold a specific article usually had the same shape wherever they were made; they often were colorful and many were decorative. Of the many that hung on the wall, long and shallow ones held candles, cutlery or brush and comb. Hanging salt boxes were narrower and had covers. A hanging box much longer than it was wide held long-stemmed pipes. Wood was the usual material, and boxes were decorated with paint, carving, simple woodworking or occasionally inlay, depending on the bent of the maker. Many surviving boxes gave such good service that only traces of paint or polychrome decoration can be seen now.

PIPE BOX is pine; long-stemmed clay pipes were placed in holes at top.

SPINNING WHEEL is a small one at which a woman sat to spin flax.

CANDLE BOX with sliding top has Pennsylvania German painted polychrome decoration.

CANDLESTAND, maple, has adjustable crossbar for two candles.

YARN WINDER, or clock reel, was a wooden device for winding thread to be spun.

LAMP, to burn whale oil, is tin made in a classic shape on a foot; wick is visible at left.

LANTERN for candle has painted pine frame, metal cap and ring.

EAGLE is carved from pine and painted; probably by Wilhelm Schimmel, Pennsylvania.

WALL BOX probably for salt, is pine with Friesian carving; painted red.

CHANDELIER of tin with holders for candles is style commonly hung in taverns.

SCONCE, China Trade, is porcelain; hand holds brass urn-shaped socket.

WALL BOX for candles is pine with Cupid's-bow edge, no cover.

Writing-arm chair with drawer. Cut-back seat, plain crest. A popular form.

Low-back armchair, Pennsylvania type; out-scrolled arms.

Bow-back, braced (two extra spindles from tailpiece to crest).

Bow-back armchair. Well-shaped seat; knuckle-carved arm ends.

Fan-back with horned crest. Turned back uprights, bobbin-turned stretcher.

Bow-back baby's high chair with arms and footrest.

Low-back with comb. Seven spindles, spiral-carved ears.

WINDSOR

The Windsor chair originated in England in the seventeenth century. First made here about 1720, it promptly became one of our most popular furniture forms and has remained so. This is not surprising since it is light, strong, comfortable and handsome, and can be used with propriety in all but the most formal rooms. Windsors are customarily painted, perhaps because they are made of several kinds of wood: the seat usually of pine, legs and stretchers of maple or birch, bent parts and spindles of oak, hickory or ash. Preferred colors are dark green and black. Except for the writing-arm Windsor, types are named according to the construction of the back; the "combs" that are added on many examples provide the comfort of a head rest. Desirability increases with the number of spindles, the vigor of the turnings, the cant of the legs and the shaping of the solid plank seat. Other forms made in the type of "stick" construction we call Windsor include settees, cradles, love seats, footstools.

Comb-back rocker, Pennsylvania type. Arrow splats.

Double-rail back with two types of spindles. Sheraton type.

Arch-back with comb. Nine spindles, braced back, H-stretcher.

Braced arch-back (one-piece back and arms). H-stretcher.

English Windsor chairs have ornamental splats, thinner seats, much less boldly raked (angled) legs; cabriole legs are early. Elm and yew are commonest woods. Center model mass-produced in early 1800s.

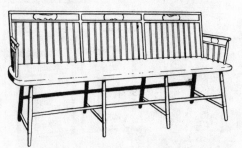

Settee. Three-chair-back Sheraton type with painted medallions; straight seat, eight legs, stretchers; each chair-back section has nine straight spindles.

Cradle. Another form using bent wood hoops and rails typical of Windsor construction.

Settee. Bow-back; curved arms with scrolled ends; bamboo-turned legs, stretchers, and arm supports.

DICTIONARY OF FURNITURE

Shaker

Worktable. Birch; two drawers, for use by two workers at a time. Tripod base, simply turned shaft.

Communal dining table. Pine top, birch trestles; used with long benches; seats 24.

Nest of boxes: a Shaker specialty. Oval shape; copper rivets hold "lappers."

Slat-back chairs. Simple finials or none; seats of splint, rush, cane or woven tape. L. to R.: high-back armchair, shop or counter chair, dining chair, high-back rocker with top rod for pad or shawl.

Sewing or tailoress table. Mixed woods stained brown; drop leaf at back.

Six-drawer chest, used as counter. Wooden drawer pulls; moldings at top and base are unusual.

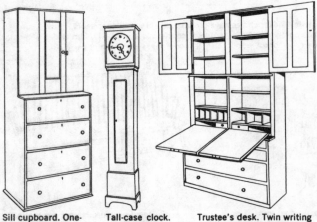

Sill cupboard. One-door cupboard set back on chest base.

Tall-case clock. Simple paneling, molding.

Trustee's desk. Twin writing surfaces, cupboards, shelves, for two working together.

COUNTRY STYLES

Several types of American furniture cannot be classified under any of the style names we have used so far. These are the pieces made in rural areas unaware of, or not impressed by, the changing fashions of the cities and larger towns. SHAKER furniture, made by members of a religious order founded in the late 1700s, is highly functional and very plain, valued for painstaking workmanship and excellent design. Like "survival" pieces, they are very difficult to date. Most of their furniture was made for their own use, but chairs for sale to the outside world were produced in impressive quantities. Gay coloring is the best-known characteristic of PENNSYLVANIA GERMAN furniture, but a lot of it is found in native walnut and other hardwoods, carved or inlaid rather than painted. Familiar motifs are tulips, hearts, stars, unicorns, birds. There is some difference of opinion as to whether these represent medieval symbolism or simply a desire to decorate. Perhaps our best-loved country style is the NEW ENGLAND, which includes some forms first made in the seventeenth century and continued, in remote districts or for common use, well into the nineteenth. Sometimes crude, it is always sturdy and often notably individualistic.

Pennsylvania German

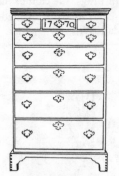 

High chest. Walnut; dated 1770; dovetails show in base.

Wardrobe (schrank). Walnut; dated and with owner's name; paneled; painted heart motif.

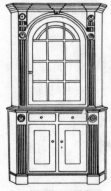 

Corner cupboard. Built in; reeded, rosetted columns, flush base.

Open-face dresser. Shelves with scrolled side pieces; base paneled; wooden door and drawer knobs.

New England

Spice box for use on shelf. Incised decoration.

Arrow-back chair. Painted green, floral decoration.

Schoolmaster's desk. Pine, old red paint; slant-front desk and two drawers on squared frame.

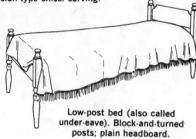

Wall box (probably for salt). Pine, painted dark green; Frisian-type chisel carving.

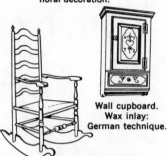

Wall cupboard. Wax inlay: German technique.

Low-post bed (also called under-eave). Block-and-turned posts; plain headboard.

High-back rocker. Early type; arched slats. Rockers often later additions.

Blanket chest. Oak with pine lid; paneled, one drawer in base, turned feet.

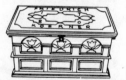

Painted chest. Tulips on front, stars in panels on side; decoration imitates inlay.

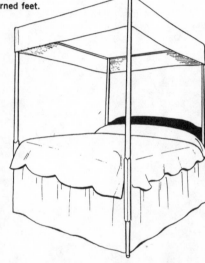

Dower chest. Painted motifs include tulips, fans, unicorns, mounted horsemen.

Open-face dresser. Flat overhanging cornice; butterfly hinges.

Drug cupboard on slant-front desk. Teardrop brasses, ball feet.

High-post bed. Maple; turned and blocked posts, curved headboard; simple canopy, no curtains.

Writing or Bible box. Paneled and gaily painted with tulips, date, owner's name.

Shelf clock. Molded, paneled; scrolled base.

Wagon-seat twin rocker. Hickory frame, rush seats; double stretcher.

Boston rocker. Black, stenciled in gilt; thick, shaped seat.

Settle chair. High back, wide wings; seat forms chest.

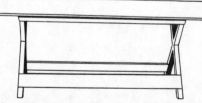

Tavern table. Drawers in two widths; heart-and-scroll carved skirt, vase-and-ring turned legs.

Tavern table. Oak and pine; oval top; canted vase-and-ring turned legs, box stretcher.

Sawbuck table. A form popular since earliest days because of strength, efficiency. Maple trestle, two-board pine top; X-shaped trestle supports, plain horizontal stretchers.